"COFFEE
— *is for* —
CLOSERS ONLY!"

"COFFEE IS FOR CLOSERS ONLY!"

TAB EDWARDS

A TAB REPORT BOOK
PUBLISHED BY OXFORD HILL PRESS

Philadelphia   New York   Chicago   Toronto

OXFORD HILL PRESS

A Division of *The Oxford Hill Consulting Group*

Copyright © 2006 by Tab M. Edwards. All rights reserved. Printed in the United States of America. Except as permitted under the United States Copyright Act of 1976, no part of this publication may be reproduced or distributed in any form or by ant means, or stored in a data base or retrieval system, without the prior written permission of the publisher.

ISBN 0-9700891-2-0; (SECOND EDITION, paper back)

This publication is designed to provide authoritative information in regards to the subject matter covered. It is sold with the understanding that the publisher is not engaged in rendering legal, accounting, or other professional services. If legal advice or other expert assistance is required, the services of a competent professional person should be sought.

—From a declaration of principles jointly adopted by a committee of the American Bar Association and a committee of publishers.

Oxford Hill Press books are available at special quantity discounts to use as premiums and sales promotions, or for use in corporate training programs. For more information, please contact Monise Gersh at monise.gersh@oxfordhill.com.

Designed by Joshua Black of Blackeyesoup.com
Philadelphia, PA.

CONTENTS

Preface VIII

PART I: THE SET UP

1. "PUT THAT COFFEE DOWN!" 03
2. WHY DO SALESPEOPLE DRINK SO MUCH COFFEE, ANYWAY? 08
3. RUN, HIDE! 12
4. LIAR, LIAR, PANTS ON FIRE! 19
5. WHAT EXACTLY *IS* "SELLING," ANYWAY? 24

PART II: THE MEAT

6. ORDER-TAKER VS. SALESMAN 31
7. THINK? KNOW? PROVE? 37
8. SELL AN ORANGE 45
9. I'LL TAKE THE RED MEAT, PLEASE! 49
10. CREDIBILITY 56
11. HANDS, FEET, AND HAIR 64
12. "SHUT THE F@#K UP!" 71

PART III: INTERMISSION

13. Intermission 78

PART IV: THE LOGIC

14. How'd He Get *HER!?* 82

CONTENTS

IV — PART IV: THE LOGIC (Continued)

15	A SERIOUS VEXATION: PERSONALITY-TYPE ANALYSES	91
16	FISHING	105
17	CHARACTERISTICS OF THE PERFECT SALES PERSON	116
18	TAB'S FIVE UNIVERSAL TRUTHS	121
19	YOU SHOULD BE OFFENDED!	132

V — PART V: THE CLOSE

20	CROSS PENS	141
21	CONCLUSION	147
22	CURTAIN CALL	153

"Everybody has a plan until they get hit.
Eventually, you're just gonna have to fight!"

MIKE TYSON, Former Heavyweight Boxing Champion

PREFACE

THINK ABOUT IT: HOW MANY TIMES IN YOUR SALES CAREER have you been introduced to yet another model for selling? Whether it's SPIN Selling, Strategic Selling, Conceptual Selling, Value-Added Selling, NFAR Selling, Relationship Selling, Customer-Focused Selling, Guerilla Selling or Voodoo Selling, it seems that every time some consultant comes up with a new twist on an old selling model, the world is again introduced to more of the same-ol'-thing — a selling model that sounds fancy, but whose practical value is questionable.

Sales trainers and consultants are beating-down the doors of sales-oriented companies advocating the acceptance of their proposals to train the company's sales force on the "latest, most cutting-edge A-then-B-then-C selling models and techniques." They sell the unsuspecting companies on the promise that by employing their latest-fad sales methodologies, the company's sales force will "increase their sales, increase their close rates and become the trusted advisors to their customers."

In all of my years of selling, consulting, and conducting sales training, I dare say that I can recall any customer ever tell the sales trainers and consultants to, "Prove it!" Sure, when asked about the effectiveness of their new selling methodologies,

PREFACE

these sales trainers can produce customer testimonials and training feedback scores out the wazoo. But does that prove that the sales training and the adoption of the sales trainer's selling methodology actually worked? Nope. The best way to validate the effectiveness of training and selling methodology-adoption is by measuring the sales reps' post-training selling proficiency this year, and measuring it again 1-year later.

But measuring something like this can be very difficult. In the early 1980's some professors at The University of Tennessee initiated the concept of Value-Added Assessment studies. This concept of value-added accountability is, in its simplest form, an attempt to measure how much someone gains from measure-1 to measure-2, and how much of the gain is attributable to different variables. Although this form of measurement is primarily used to measure a student's academic progress, the concept can be applicable to a broader body of study, including sales proficiency.

Conducting value-added assessments can be technically complicated. What do you measure: Quota attainment? Customer satisfaction? Product-line growth? Margin improvement? Cost-per-order-dollar (CPOD)? Sales process knowledge? Business plan knowledge? As you can imagine, this is not an easy thing to do and, therefore, I don't believe that many (if any) companies have ever really invested in performing such rigorous analyses. And if that is true (which I believe it is), then no one really knows or can prove that these selling strategies and methodologies actually work. [See Chapter 7: Think? Know? Prove? Honesty in the Sales Cycle]. And if no one can prove that following these strategies actually deliver

PREFACE

the promised results, then why do companies spend so much money each year training their sales forces on them?

Okay, I'll be among the first to acknowledge that there is *some* value in understanding the fundamentals of selling as the foundation for your selling motion. I believe that such things as basic objection handling, listening & questioning skills, conceptual selling, strategic selling, customer-focused selling, and many other fundamental sales training activities can be quite helpful for new sales reps because they give you a foundation to fall-back on when you get lost in the sales cycle. But beyond that, there is scant evidence to prove that non-fundamental sales methodologies deliver on the promises.

Most of these esoteric sales techniques and strategies sound reasonable in theory, but it's the practical application where many of them fall short.

For example, there are tons of books on the market that offer advice on "How to Pick up Women." They all claim to work and they all guarantee that you will increase your pick-up rate by following these techniques. They even offer a long list of customer testimonials! Below are two of my favorites. According to one self-proclaimed so-called *pick-up artist*, they are two of the top three tips for picking up women, and by employing these techniques, "you will attract women like a magnet!"

1. TEASE HER WITH ATTENTION "(This one is just dirty!). While you are macking on a particular girl, go away after you've talked for a while and begin talking to someone else. Just say to her: "I need to disappear for a bit, I'll be back." Try to make it a male friend that you go talk to, or she will think you're a player... (let's make that OUR secret, ok?). This will drive her crazy, and if you've made a decent impression on her, she won't be able to think of anything except you – and when you are going to come back. Some of the bolder females out there may even come and butt into your new conversation. However, if she does not, go back after a short period of time and you will notice that she will be ten times more into you than she was before!"

2. THE SEDUCTIVE SMILE. "Upon making eye contact with a woman that you are interested in, always smile. I'm not talking about one of those huge "say cheese" smiles, rather, a smirk (maybe a little bit more than a smirk) that says "I'm happy you've looked at me." Once smiling, hold the gaze for 1-2 seconds, then look away. After looking away, try to get her to make eye contact with you again, if this happens go over and talk to her, because her second look was your invitation."

As any man or woman can tell you, there's more to "picking-up" someone than following such [your adjective here] techniques. You could follow these pick-up-artist methodologies to the letter, but if 50 other things don't fall into place, then you're not gonna pick-up anyone! Not to mention that once you are actually engaged in discussion with that person, the conversation may take such a course that following your script becomes impossible — and then you're *just gonna have to fight!*

The same is true for selling. You can follow these fancy selling techniques as prescribed, but if a host of other conditions are not met, then you won't get the sale [See Chapter 16: *Fishing*].

The purpose of this book is to share some observations and thoughts on the profession of selling, and to do so in a tongue-

PREFACE

in-cheek manner. It is not intended as an instructional manual or a "how-to-sell" book — believe me, there are enough of those out there. Besides, you'll never learn to be a good salesperson by simply reading a book. *Coffee is for Closers Only!* is intended to entertain while providing some usable substance.

Some of the ideas I share throughout this book will, I'm sure, be seen as controversial, and you will undoubtedly not agree with everything I write herein; I don't expect you to. I don't know of too many people that *do* agree with everything they read — except, maybe members of a cult. So I expect you to question what you read in this book and to ask yourself whether the ideas are reasonable or not. It they are reasonable, then maybe you'll find some value in them; if not, then blow it off ... move on to the next topic.

The purpose of the book is not to discredit text-book selling techniques and strategies, but to take the alternate position that, for the experienced seller, the value of many of the new-fangled sales techniques is questionable at best, and that sellers should focus on certain foundational aspects of selling in order to improve their effectiveness. But you be the judge ...

PART ONE
THE SET-UP

"Relative deprivation is the experience of being deprived of something to which one thinks he is entitled to."

WALKER & SMITH

CH01.

"PUT THAT COFFEE DOWN!"

"COFFEE IS FOR CLOSERS ONLY!"

AMONG THE ALL-TIME GREAT SALES MOVIES, *Glengarry Glen Ross* has to be at the top of any true salesperson's list. It's one of the few movies with the sales profession as a central theme that accurately captures the angst, cunning, duplicity and desperation of the gritty salesman.

For the two of you out there who haven't seen the movie, *Glengarry Glen Ross* tells the story of four Real Estate property salesmen including Sheldon "Shelley" Levene (Jack Lemmon) and Ricky "Roma" (Al Pacino). The salesmen work for a company called Rio Rancho (or Consolidated Properties or any of the other names they tell their prospects) and they are all — with the exception of Roma — well under quota. The owners of the company, some guys named "Mitch & Murray," are concerned by the underperformance of the salesmen and decide to send an intimidator to the sales office to kick the salesmen in the butt and get them motivated to work harder. The intimidator, "Blake" (Alec Baldwin), is a stranger in the office and no one knows who he is and what he is there for. All the salesmen know is that they have been called into a mandatory emergency meeting that will start at "7:30PM sharp."

Nobody knows who Blake is, but he's moving around the manager's office like he owns the place. Blake then moves onto the sales floor. He's wearing the most powerful of power suits and he looks like a million-bucks. He turns to the salesmen and abruptly launches into a diatribe and delivers the most belittling speech you can imagine; he is both intimidating and arrogant. He starts by yelling at the men to get their "minds off unimportant things like family and supper and the weekend."

PART ONE: THE SET UP

"Instead," he says, "let's talk about something important!" Just then, he notices that Shelley is pouring himself a cup of coffee. "Put that coffee down!" he orders. "Coffee is for closers only!" Shelley looks at him, incredulous. "You think I'm f@#king with you?" he asks Shelley. "Well, I am *not* f@#king with you!" Shelley puts down the cup of coffee. Blake continues, "I'm here from downtown. I'm here for Mitch & Murray, and I'm here on a mission of mercy." He looks at Shelley and asks, "Your name's Levene?" Shelley replies, "Yeah." To which Blake responds, "You call yourself a *salesman*, you son-of-a-bitch?"

He continues to berate the men: "If you can't close the leads you are given, you can't close *sh#t*, you *are* sh#t!" Then Shelley chimes in, "The leads are weak!" To which Blake shouts, "The *leads* are weak?! F@#kin' *leads* are weak?! *You're* weak!"

The brow-beating continues: "… only one thing counts in this life – get them to sign on the line which is dotted!" Blake then walks over to the chalk board and reads: *"A, B, C: A–Always, B–Be, C–Closing. Always Be Closing!"* Classic cinema and a classic sales phrase!

To me, Blake's earlier statement is one of the great lines of any movie I have seen — *"Coffee is for closers only!"* The Alec Baldwin character goes to the extreme when it comes to threatening the salesmen in order to get them to perform better, and he does it to perfection. Although I believe his tactics were brutal and way over the top, on some levels I agree with the point he was making by denying Shelley a cup of coffee. That point being: what have you done lately to deserve any perks?

"COFFEE IS FOR CLOSERS ONLY!"

Far too often sales professionals are rewarded for doing absolutely *nothing*. In my twenty-plus years of experience I have seen clueless salespeople reap the rewards of someone who has mastered his craft, performed a spectacular selling job, and closed millions of dollars worth of business over quota, all because they were either at the right place at the right time, worked for companies that didn't pay based on individual performance, and/or were part of a team where they could get away with having absolutely nothing to contribute. More-and-more, however, companies are starting to remove the shields that these salespeople hide behind, and are forcing them to prove that they are worthy of that "cup of coffee."

Unfortunately, what companies are finding when they remove these shields is that many of their sales representatives lack the fundamental selling skills necessary to be effective at their jobs. And even with the sales reps who understand the fundamentals of selling, many of them struggle when it comes to calling on executives, selling solutions, and being more consultative in their approach.

The primary purpose of this book is to share with you some ideas that experience and research have proven can make someone a better sales person —while keeping you entertained along the read. This book is neither offered as a selling fundamentals book, nor is it intended to be a *how-to* or an instructional manual. So if you are looking for "the basics of selling," then I dare say that you're out 12-bucks!

And speaking of a cup of coffee ...

"The morning cup of coffee has an exhilaration about it which the cheering influence of the afternoon or evening cup of tea cannot be expected to reproduce."

OLIVER WENDELL HOLMES, *"Over the Teacups,"* **1891**

CH02.

WHY DO SALESPEOPLE DRINK SO MUCH COFFEE, *ANYWAY!?*

PART ONE: THE SET UP

IN AN OCTOBER 2005 SURVEY COMMISSIONED BY *BUSINESS WEEK,* findings from a survey of 25-45 year olds showed that 77% of the respondents make coffee at home regularly, and 24% drink 13-cups of coffee or more each week. In addition, more than 50% of Americans drink coffee every day — three to four cups each, and more than 330 million cups-per-day overall. And if I had to guess, I would assume that the numbers for sales professionals is twice that amount. What's up with that? Why do salespeople drink so much coffee?

Well, for one thing, the sales profession can be depressing. It also requires stamina and mental alertness. And one legal way to get that jolt of energy to refresh and stimulate yourself for your round of afternoon calls is with a few swigs of coffee with caffeine.

Caffeine is an alkaloid drug (contained in coffee and tea) that has a stimulant action, particularly on the central nervous system. It is used to promote wakefulness and increase mental activity. This is the reason I believe so many salespeople like coffee — not for the taste, but for the *caffeine*; it's addictive and it's legal. Is it merely a coincidence that the most popular drinks in the world (soda, coffee, tea) all contain caffeine? I dunno, but I doubt it.

Another attractive characteristic of caffeinated-coffee is that it is fast-acting; it is absorbed by the body within minutes. Then, once absorbed, the caffeine from the coffee blocks adenosine (a chemical that tells the brain that the body is tired), and suddenly the body thinks it is refreshed and energetic. That's the "high" or the "buzz" that caffeinated-coffee drinkers talk about, and it's what makes them crave the drink

"COFFEE IS FOR CLOSERS ONLY!"

even more.

    Every day it seems that we are hearing more and more about the benefits of caffeine: it picks you up, it makes you more alert, and it elevates your mood. That mood-elevation benefit (a.k.a. "high") is the one that I'm sure many salespeople crave after being beaten-up — or shall I say, beaten *down* — by customers all day.

"Most people have experienced buyer's remorse in some form, whether it's feeling guilty over the price paid for a new pair of shoes or a jab of regret after splurging on some unneeded tech gizmo."

AMY HOAK, MarketWatch

CH03.

RUN, HIDE!

PART ONE: THE SET UP

IN ALL THE WORLD OF BUSINESS TRANSACTIONS, THERE IS ONE UGLY TRUTH: *NOBODY LIKES TO DEAL WITH SALES PEOPLE!*

How many other professions can boast that when someone sees you coming they try to avoid you? The Bounty Hunter? The Truant Officer, maybe? The list is short. And there is something inherently insulting about that, too. Think about it: you spend thousands of dollars attending the finest schools and universities; you go out and buy the most expensive suits so that you look good on your job interviews; you waste countless hour reading those "how to sell" books; you spend your precious time attending sales classes; and you finally land a sales job at a prestigious Fortune-500 Company – *only to have customers and prospects pretend they're out of the office when you call!!*

Why is that? How did that "fear of the salesman" become consistent behavior not just in the business world, but in every walk of life? When and how did it all begin? What causes sales resistance? Some people theorize that the answer lies in the nature of selling.

But let's step back for a second. Universal truth: everyone loves money. And because we love money so much, we hate to part with it – especially for something we're not sure we wanted to buy in the first place. Universal truth: nobody likes to be forced to do something they don't want to do. Sales people have a reputation for convincing us to buy things that we later regret purchasing (more on that later in this chapter). In other words, they force us to do things we later regret and to part with our money in the process – a double-whammy!

So, I believe that a big part of our reluctance to deal with pushy salespeople is because of our experience with buyer's remorse. That's not a pleasant feeling.

Ok, now for a more technical theory of why people have a resistance to salespeople. When asked, surveys show that people offer any number of reasons why they don't like dealing with salespeople, including pressure tactics, past experience, and lies & deceit. I've got a secret to share with all of you sales reps out there: *you're a saleaperson and everyone knows that your job is to sell them something!* And any attempt to cover up the fact that you're trying to sell us something gives buyers the perception of dishonesty which makes them feel like they're being conned or ripped-off.

People know that your job is to get them to part with their money, and — as some people believe – to do so by all means, including pressure tactics, laying guilt trips and down-right lying. And when a person believes that you are trying to get them to do something they don't want to do, then that relationship immediately becomes antagonistic and forces the buyer to put up his or her guard and go into defensive mode. And by definition, personal selling involves someone buying something from a salesperson, which means that even before the first discussion takes place, the sales rep is already at a perceptual negative starting position in the eyes of the prospective buyer.

But I have another theory of why no one likes dealing with salespeople: *Quota!* It probably happened something like this:

"Selling" is the world's oldest profession. I know, I know

PART ONE: THE SET UP

... we've always been told that *prostitution* is the oldest profession. But when you think about it, in a competitive market, the prostitute had to be an adept sales person to get customers. She (or he) had to "sell" the deal before the merchandise exchange and financial transaction (the "close") took place. So selling has been going on *forever*.

I imagine that one day some inventive soul — who was faced with a problem — created something that solved the problem, made life easier or provided some level of comfort. He'd soon realize that his neighbors could use his invention to solve their problems, too. News would travel throughout the colony that some guy has created something that makes life so much more bearable. Before long, people from far & wide would seek out the product that the inventive soul created. But the inventive soul's resources were limited and he couldn't possibly make enough of the product to give to everyone who asked.

Learning that there was a shortage of the product, some desperate product-seekers would offer the inventive soul money (or cow-chips or yak teeth or whatever form of currency was used at that time) as an inducement to make his or her request for the product a priority. Suddenly, the inventive soul realized he could become a wealthy man by *sel0ling* his product instead of giving it away for free!

After months of selling his product, the inventive soul was now a wealthy man. But there was a problem. It turns out that everyone in the colony who needed the product had the product, which meant that there was no longer a market for his product in the colony. This was a problem because the

"COFFEE IS FOR CLOSERS ONLY!"

inventive soul had grown accustomed to the new lifestyle he had achieved and he needed more money to continue living that way. The only way he knew to make money was by selling his product, and the only way he could sell his product was by traveling to other colonies and peddling his wares to the people there; thus was born the *traveling salesman.*

But traveling from colony-to-colony on the back of a brontosaurus was not easy, so the inventive soul recruited other people to sell his product for him. The inventive soul calculated that he had to sell 100 pieces of his product monthly to maintain his luxurious lifestyle. So he hired ten out-of-work farmers (the first *sales reps*) and told them that if they each sold 10 pieces of the product within a month's time, then, and only then, would they be paid a percentage of the take—*the first sales quota!* The idea worked, and the inventive soul went on to live a prosperous life.

Over time, other colonists saw that they, too, could become wealthy like the inventive soul, so all kinds of products were being invented and sold—some good, and most bad. These new inventors followed the sales rep/sales quota model created by the inventive soul. There were so many products springing up that the competition for the scarce consumer dollar (cow chip) was fierce. In order to get a leg up on the competition so that they could make their monthly quota, many sales reps would make outrageous, false claims about the benefits of their product in order to beat the competition—thus was born *the marketing guy!*

Outrageously false claims became the norm. I can imagine that people started creating products that offered no benefit at

PART ONE: THE SET UP

all. They realized that they could get people to buy the product based on the false benefits the product was said to deliver. This false advertising approach had its downside though, because when buyers learned that the product was bogus, they tracked-down the lying salesman and beat him to a pulp!

Some slick salesmen realized that if they joined a traveling circus that went from town-to-town, they could con people into buying these bogus products and skip town before the buyers realized the products didn't work as advertised. That way, they could make a ton of money and be long-gone before the ass-whuppers hunted them down.

Back in those days, snake-oil somehow became the bogus product du jour. After all, it could, "Cure what ails ya!" [I know this sentence doesn't really fit here, but I really wanted to include it, and this looked as safe a place as any].

Needless to say, these traveling salesmen had a terrible reputation and were the most un-trustworthy of all professionals. Whenever a salesman came-a-callin' they were either summarily dismissed or greeted with a suspecting eye of caution.

This reputation soon shifted from only *traveling* salesmen, to *salesmen* in general. The feeling was then—and is now—that sales people will try to pressure you into buying something that is bogus or something that you don't want or need just so that they can make their sales quota; I'm sure we've all seen examples of that in our experiences. And even though a high percentage of sales professionals are reasonably honest sellers, people still hate dealing with salespeople. Think about it. Do *you* like being called on by sales people?

"It is hard to tell if a man is telling the truth when you know you would lie if you were in his place."

H.L. MENCKEN, Author

CH04.

LIAR, LIAR, PANTS ON FIRE!

"COFFEE IS FOR CLOSERS ONLY!"

ONE OF MY UNIVERSAL TRUTHS IS: NO SALES REP "LOVES" TO SELL, and any of those annoyingly-bubbly, overly-enthusiastic phonies who say they do are lying! Let's be honest, folks. Like I always say — "We are only sales reps because *we got the job.*" Because if – when we were out interviewing for jobs — someone offered us a job as a *meat inspector* (making the same money as the sales rep) we would all be meat inspectors. Not because we "love" inspecting meat, but because *we got the job!*

Some people say that they are sales reps because of the earning potential — makes sense. Some people say they are sales reps because they like being out on the road — makes sense. Some people say they are sales reps because it's easy to get a sales job — makes sense. Some people say they are sales reps because certain types of sales reps have a reputation of being savvy – makes sense. But some people say they are sales reps because they "love" to sell — *bulls@#t!*

Saying you "love" to sell is like saying you "love" rejection, belittlement, having an inferiority complex, high stress, looking for a job every couple of years, chasing quota, and that you love waking up on Monday mornings. And I'm sure that nobody "loves" *that*. Yeah, I know … that's only *my* educated opinion. But don't just take my word for it – the proof is in the pudding. Let's take a few minutes to consider a few things. If selling is so "wonderful" as to make people "love" to do it, then:

- Why do approximately 85% of the people who become sales reps leave the profession within the first few years? Because it's so *loveable*? I doubt it.

PART ONE: THE SET UP

- Name one other profession that comes with a built-in expectation of rejection.
- How many other professions have had "do not call" legislation passed against them restricting sales reps from calling peoples' homes?
- Why do the majority of customers and prospects refuse to talk to you (or do so begrudgingly) when they find out that you are selling something?
- Why do companies hire consultants to come in and subject you to serious amounts of motivational psychology in hopes of inspiring you to go out and sell? Who else does this?
- Why does the sales profession spend the most money of any other profession on motivational training? Only the military is a close competitor, and they have to go out and face far greater risks and stressful situations than simply calling on *customers*!

So, you think I'm off my rocker? That there are some people out there who actually *do* love to sell? Then here's a test for anyone who says they *love* to sell: Imagine that you inherited $20 Million from a long-lost uncle that you didn't even know existed. The uncle left you the inheritance under one condition: You must do some type of productive work — in other words, you can do any type of work you want to do, whether it's pursuing your hobby as wine-maker, becoming a photographer, becoming a chef, writing books or becoming a florist ... *anything*. But you cannot just take the money and go on a

"COFFEE IS FOR CLOSERS ONLY!"

10-year vacation. The question is: Under these circumstances, how many of you would keep your jobs as a *salesman?!?* Just as I suspected, ZERO!

The logic is that people presented with this scenario — under which they can do *anything* they want and not have to worry about a paycheck — will opt to do something they *love* to do. And if *no one* says they would continue to schlep a bag, chase quota, and deal with irate customers, then *no one* really *loves* to sell.

Okay. Let me back-track a little. I can't say that *nobody* "loves" to sell. After all, some people "love" eating maggots, some people "love" to be whipped & tortured, some people "love" hairless cats, and some people even "love" rapper Vanilla Ice. So maybe there are people who actually "love" to sell. I just haven't met any.

"Everyone lives by selling something."
ROBERT LOUIS STEVENSON, Scottish novelist, poet

CH05.

WHAT, EXACTLY *IS* "SELLING," ANYWAY?

PART ONE: THE SET UP

THERE ARE PROBABLY HUNDREDS OF DEFINITIONS of what it means to "*sell.*" For instance, Purdue University puts forth this definition of selling:

Selling is a process – helping people access the Products, Services, and Information needed to meet personal and business goals. They also say: *it involves person-to-person interaction.*

Another definition states: *Knowledge of the customer's business – whether cows or computers, flowers or database management – is the basis of a good decision. And good decisions allow continued business with each customer.*

According to Webster's Dictionary, selling is *the exchange of a product or service for money; to offer something for sale.* (Did anyone else catch that faux paux in this definition? Weren't we taught in 3rd grade not to use the word we are trying to *define* in the definition of that word? It's kinda like defining a "dog" as: a *dog* that walks on four legs. Anyway ...).

Technically, this definition of *selling* is probably correct, however, I have a different view of what it means to "sell" as a profession. Tab's definition:

> *Selling* is the art of extracting and clearly defining those things which challenge a person's comfortable existence, and gaining his or her confidence that you have access to "something" that will alleviate the discomfort, while persuading the person to believe that what you have is better for the person than anything anyone else can provide; It is *"the art of movement"* – moving a person to believe as you want them to be-

25

lieve, and to behave as you want them to behave.

As I stated above, I believe selling is the art of *"movement."* It is the art of taking a person from some initial position or mindset and "moving" them to a position where they share your vision and accept your recommendation because they believe it to be in their best interest.

Based on my experience as a salesman selling in various situations to companies of various types, sizes, complexities and markets, I believe a person only really *sells* when at least three conditions exist:

1. **THERE MUST BE AN ELEMENT OF PERSUASION INVOLVED; YOU MUST CONVINCE SOMEONE TO SEE YOUR POINT OF VIEW.**

   As a seller, you must convince a person to realize they need your offering even when they don't fully initially realize they need it, or when they initially tell you they don't want your offering. For whatever reason – like the old axiom goes – "Selling doesn't begin until the customer says 'NO'."

2. **FORMIDABLE COMPETITIVE OFFERINGS MUST EXIST AND MUST BE KNOWN AND AVAILABLE TO THE PROSPECT.**

   If you are the only game in town, then a customer or prospect has no choice except to buy your offering. This is not selling, because, according to my definition of selling, you don't have to convince the prospect that your offering is better for them than anything anyone else can provide. If a customer has viable options available to him or her, you are then required to engage in the art of persuasion. For instance, if you live in a small hick town with only one general store and that store only sells Nike sneakers, then you, as the Nike salesman at the store, don't have to convince the sneaker-buying customer to purchase the Nike brand – they have no choice; no selling required.

3. **THE PROSPECT OR CUSTOMER MUST BE RELUCTANT TO MEET WITH YOU BECAUSE THEY DON'T WANT TO HAVE "SOME SALESPERSON BUGGING THEM ABOUT SPENDING MONEY."**

A big part of the sales process is convincing a prospect to give you the opportunity to tell your story. If the situation exists where the prospect is reluctant to meet with you, your salesmanship comes into play as you try to tell the prospect why it would be of value for him or her to meet with you. On the other hand, if a prospect or customer actively solicits a meeting with you, they are either interested in buying what you have to sell, or, at a minimum, are interested in being convinced to buy what you have to sell. In this situation, very little selling (if any) is involved, and your role will be more *information-provider*, and less *seller*.

I believe that order-taker status is not necessarily a permanent distinction; we've all had those moments in our career when we did little-to-no selling and still walked away with an order from our customers. And I will admit that it's not necessary to really *sell* for every opportunity. The problem with the order-taker is that they can only be successful when no real *selling* is involved. As soon as they are confronted with a competitive sales situation that requires a deal to be worked all throughout the account and at all levels of management — where the product itself is almost irrelevant — they can't adjust. And in these situations, they will inevitably lose the deal to a competitive seller who — with a viable product or solution alternative— knows how to *sell*.

PART TWO
THE MEAT

"Show me a sales rep that achieves his or her annual quota target while never calling on executives, and I'll show you an order-taker."

TAB EDWARDS, Consultant, Author

CH06.

ORDER-TAKER vs. SALESMAN

"COFFEE IS FOR CLOSERS ONLY!"

ANY SALESPERSON WORTH HIS OR HER SALT WOULD TAKE OFFENSE to being called an "order-taker." Being called an *order-taker* implies that the salesperson is lazy, plays golf all day, doesn't really do any selling, doesn't know how to sell, and is stealing money from their company because they are adding no *value* to their companies.

A simple example to help explain the concept of *value* is the Internet purchase: Suppose a customer wants to buy a high-definition television. The customer can go to a store's web site to order it on-line, or the customer can visit the store in person — where the price of the television is 3% higher — and buy the television with the assistance of a sales person. If the customer elects to go to the store to benefit from the advice of the sales person, then that customer sees value in that sales person, because he/she is willing to travel to the store and pay 3% more for the same television he/she could have purchased on-line.

The line between that which distinguishes an "order-taker" from a "salesman" (I will use this term to include all sales *persons*) is, understandably, quite blurred. The reality is that anyone who holds the title of "Sales Representative," or "Account Executive," or "Sales Specialist," or "Account Manager," or "Marketing Representative," or any of the other titles given to those in a selling capacity (more on the definition of *selling* later) considers him or herself to be a salesman. But when they do this, they are oftentimes giving themselves too much credit. There *is* a difference between an "order-taker" and a real "salesman."

PART TWO: THE MEAT

YOU MIGHT BE AN ORDER-TAKER IF ...

- If you were removed as the salesperson from your set of accounts or territory and your customers continued to buy the same amount of your product or service (+/- 5%) as the did when you were their sales rep on the account, then you might just be an order-taker. For example. John sells office paper to Company A — his primary account. For the last 5 years straight, John has been recognized by his company as a top salesman by always exceeding his annual quota; last year his quota was $5,000,000 and he sold $7,000,000 worth of paper to Company A. Well John began "smelling himself" a little, so he quit his job to go work for a competitor at a higher salary. John's co-worker, Mary, took over responsibility for the Company A account. Mary was a capable sales rep, but she had failed to achieve her quota in each of the last 3 years. But ever since being assigned to Company A, she has been crushing her quota; this year she sold $9,000,000 worth of office paper to Company A.

The point I want to make by this example is that John added no value to Company A when he had it as an account. The fact that the sales didn't decrease when he left shows that in all likelihood, he was an order-taker. This is supported by the fact that underachieving-Mary was able to grow the business (or shall I say – take more orders) at the account when she took over.

- If 50% or more of the dollar value of the deals you closed this year are the result of your customer(s) calling you in

"COFFEE IS FOR CLOSERS ONLY!"

to discuss an opportunity or to tell you what they are interested in buying from you (including the issuance of an RFP), then you might just be an order-taker.

- If your customer calls you and tells you that she wants to buy $200,000 worth of your company's paper cups, and you accept the order without asking the customer why she wants to purchase the cups, then you just might me an order-taker.

- If you spend the majority of your selling time calling on customers who are four-levels or more removed from the company's President — and you still achieve your sales quota each year — then you just might be an order-taker.

- If your customer can buy your commodity products just as effectively from you as they can from a 3rd party's website, then you just might be an order-taker. For example. If you were buying a coffee mug and you had a choice to order it from Amazon.com or to have a salesman visit your house to sell you one, you would surely opt to buy the cup on-line. And let's suppose you needed to buy large quantities of the coffee mugs and you had a few questions. You would probably either check the company's website for information on the product, or you would place a phone call to the coffee mug sales rep to get the necessary information. Once satisfied with the answer, you'd then just simply place the order with the sales rep over the phone. Admittedly, that's a simplistic scenario, but the reality is that as products become commoditized and companies create e-commerce portals, the role of the commodity sales rep becomes less

PART TWO: THE MEAT

significant and akin to an order-taker.

Sometimes, the nature of the products or services you sell, or the status of your product in the marketplace relative to that of your competitors' can dictate that your selling motion defines you as an order-taker. Say, for instance, the year is 1967 and you are an IBM sales representative. Back then, IBM was basically the only game in town, and if customers wanted to purchase or rent a mainframe (big) computer system, they had to get it from IBM because no other company had anything of the kind. I often heard the stories from some of the IBM sales reps of that era about how great it was to just sit back and take the orders. Those sales reps were admitted order-takers.

Another example of the product dictating the order-taker status of a sales rep could be something like metal clothes-hangers; if you want some, call me, because mine are just like his. I don't imagine there is a whole helluva lot of true selling that goes into the sale of metal clothes-hangers. That's probably one of those products were price and trust in the company (e.g. the ability to deliver the quantity needed on-time, a good relationship with the company, etc.) account for more deals getting done than the savvy of a sales person.

I'm not gonna sit here and pretend that all good sales reps "sell" all of the time – they don't. We've all been the beneficiary of *bluebirds* and order-taking throughout our careers; it's the nature of the profession. However, when a good salesperson *has* to "sell," they have the wherewithal to go out and get the business.

"If it is a *Miracle*, any sort of evidence will answer, but if it is a *Fact*, proof is necessary."

MARK TWAIN

CH07.

THINK? KNOW? PROVE?

HONESTY IN THE SALES CYCLE

"COFFEE IS FOR CLOSERS ONLY!"

THERE ARE TWO COMMON PERSPECTIVES ON WHAT WE COMMONLY REFER TO AS THE SALES CYCLE: The sales rep's view and from the buyer's perspective.

From the *buyer's perspective*, the sales cycle can be seen as the sequence of stages that a typical *customer* goes through when deciding to buy something; this is the sales cycle from the *customer's* perspective. This perspective is also known as the *buying cycle,* and describes the typical process (or stages) that we all go through when we buy something. The stages include:

1. Identification of a need, whether real or perceived
2. Investigation of potential solutions to satisfy the need
3. Evaluation of the alternatives
4. Making the purchase decision

From the *seller's perspective*, the sales cycle looks a little different. There are umpteen different versions of what the sales cycle looks like from the seller's perspective, most of which conform to a consistent model of what are considered to be the common stages that sales reps go through in the pursuit of a deal.

The *Stages to the Sale* that I propose is consistent with other models of the selling cycle, however, I include additional no-brainer stages at the beginning of the process, and more "honesty-checking" activities throughout the process as described below.

PART TWO: THE MEAT

STAGES TO THE SALE

1. IDENTIFY A PROSPECT
2. GAIN ACCESS TO THE PROSPECT
3. DETERMINE OR CONFIRM THE EXISTENCE OF AN OPPORTUNITY
4. QUALIFY THE OPPORTUNITY USING THE T-K-P CONCEPT
    a. Do I THINK there is an opportunity? Do I KNOW there is an opportunity? Can I PROVE there is a real opportunity?
5. UNDERSTAND THE TRUE REQUIREMENTS
    a. Do I THINK I understand the customer's true requirements? Do I KNOW what the customer's true requirements are? Can I PROVE that I know what the customer's true requirements are?
6. DEVELOP A POTENTIAL SOLUTION & SOLUTION JUSTIFICATION
7. QUALIFY THE SOLUTION
    a. Do I THINK the solution will deliver the expected benefits, do I KNOW it, can I PROVE it?
    b. Do I THINK the customer will buy the value of the solution, do I KNOW it, can I PROVE it?
    c. Does the customer have funds allocated to pay for the solution?
    d. Have I sold the solution to the signatory of the deal and other players?
8. PRESENT THE SOLUTION PROPOSAL
9. CLOSE THE DEAL AND GET THE SIGNED ORDER

"COFFEE IS FOR CLOSERS ONLY!"

The honesty-checking activities to which I refer introduce the *"Think? Know? Prove?"* (T-K-P) concept and are designed to force an added level of diligence and rigor to critical phases in the sales cycle. What we *Think* (what we believe or suppose), our level of *Knowledge* (familiarity, awareness, or understanding gained through experience or study) and that for which we have *Proof* (the act of validating; finding or testing the truth of something) can be used as measures of the level of diligence we apply to the stages of the sales cycle.

In my opinion, subjecting certain aspects of the sales cycle to this rigor helps sales reps get an honest view of where they may need to do more work before they can have a clear and honest assessment of their prospect of moving a deal to closure. Stages that pass the T-K-P rigor are, in my opinion, more credible when presented to management.

In the fields of scientific enquiry, researchers often form hypotheses in the early stages of their quests for answers and solutions to problems. As information becomes available, researchers will often apply the T-K-P check against the data and other suggestions to help decide whether or not the data qualify for consideration.

For example, let's assume that some research scientist was fed up with listening to vegetarians rant about how they only eat vegetables because they could never harm another living creature. So, in order to silence those vegetarians, the scientist developed a hypothesis that he has always believed: *Plants are living "creatures" that feel pain, too.* Applying the T-K-P rule against this hypothesis, you get the following:

HYPOTHESIS: PLANTS ARE LIVING CREATURES THAT FEEL PAIN

1. What do you THINK? I think that plants feel pain
2. What do you KNOW? We know that plants, including vegetables, feel pain when subjected to trauma such as being yanked out of the ground, peeled, cooked, and eaten.
3. What can you PROVE? Vegetables and plants initiate a massive hormone and chemical barrage internally when they suffer any kind of injury. This response is akin to the nerve response and endorphin release when an animal is injured.

If we applied this same concept to the stages of the sales cycle, it would look something like this:

STAGE #7: QUALIFY THE SOLUTION

a. Do I THINK the solution will deliver the expected benefits? Yes

b. Do I KNOW the solution will deliver the expected benefits? Yes, because we sold the same solution to Company ABC, and it delivered the same benefits that we have promised to this customer.

c. Can I PROVE the solution will deliver the expected benefits? No, because we have not piloted or test marketed the solution at this customer's location. A pilot of the solution will give us the proof that the solution will (or will not) deliver the expected benefits for this company. [This could be a red flag].

This example illustrates the level of diligence that must be applied at various stages of the sales cycle where the T-K-P test is recommended. It forces the sales rep to be honest about the prospects of selling a deal based on the degree to which all of the possible areas of customer objection have been considered and addressed.

Although the two perspectives of the sales cycle appear to be different, they should, in fact, be considered in parallel (Table A). In my experience, it has proven most effective to pursue the deal following my recommended *Stages of the Sale* or any sales cycle process, while ensuring that you are addressing the customer's buying cycle in the process.

Does following my *Stages to the Sales* cycle ensure that you will close every deal? 90% of the deals? 75% of the deals? No, it doesn't guarantee *anything*. But what it will do is provide a deal-pursuit framework that, if followed, will improve qualification (sidebar: according to research, 64% of sales managers believe that their sales reps do not qualify leads as well as they should, and 56% agree that time is wasted pursuing poor sales leads and opportunities) and increase the odds that you have left no stone unturned which will, in turn, help reduce the odds of failure due to lack of thoroughness and preparation.

PART TWO: THE MEAT

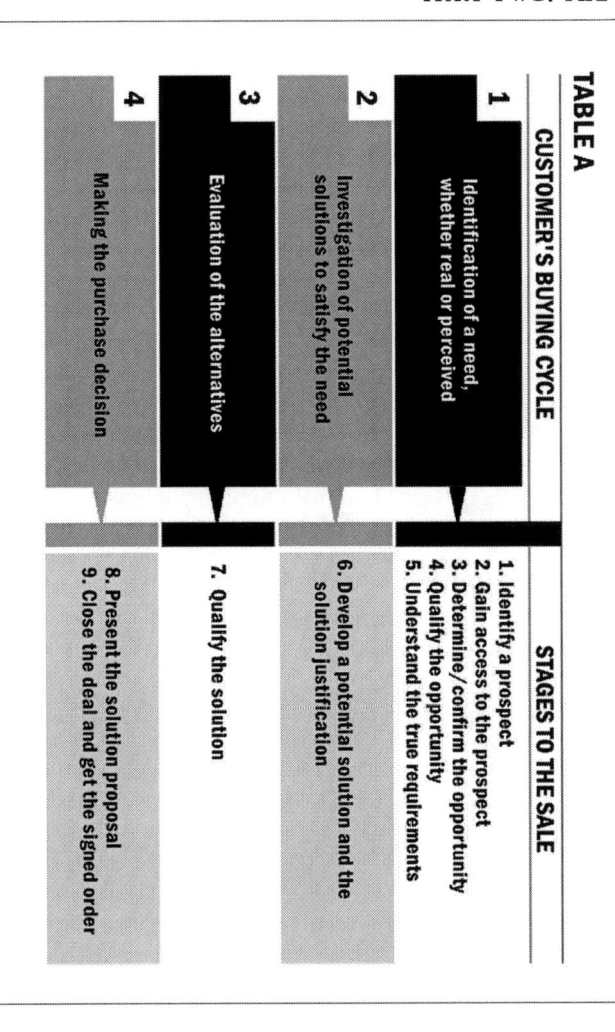

TABLE A

CUSTOMER'S BUYING CYCLE	STAGES TO THE SALE
1. Identification of a need, whether real or perceived	1. Identify a prospect 2. Gain access to the prospect 3. Determine/confirm the opportunity 4. Qualify the opportunity 5. Understand the true requirements
2. Investigation of potential solutions to satisfy the need	6. Develop a potential solution and the solution justification
3. Evaluation of the alternatives	7. Qualify the solution
4. Making the purchase decision	8. Present the solution proposal 9. Close the deal and get the signed order

43

"What the people in business think they know about the customer and market is likely to be more wrong than right. The customer rarely buys what the business thinks it sells him."

PETER DRUCKER, Management Consultant

CH08.

SELL AN ORANGE

"COFFEE IS FOR CLOSERS ONLY!"

SCENARIO: ASSUME YOU ARE AN ORANGE SALESPERSON. No ... you are not *colored* orange, but you *sell* oranges — the fruit. You have been granted a one-minute meeting with a prospective orange consumer. You have only one orange to sell and the prospect – if interested – will only care to buy one orange. How would you conduct the call?

Tests show that the majority of sales reps would approach the call by telling the prospect about all of the attributes of the orange: it's tasty, it's refreshing, it has vitamin C and fiber, it's round, etc. And before they realize it, they have spent the entire minute talking about that orange.

Let's step back for a minute and answer a few questions:

QUESTION #1: What do you do with an orange? Answer: You eat it
QUESTION #2: Why do we eat? Answer: To stave off hunger (fundamentally)
QUESTION #3: When do we eat? Answer: When we're hungry

So, if you were trying to sell the prospect the orange it would make sense to determine whether or not the prospect was hungry. If the prospect had just eaten a 7-course meal, then chances are she would not be hungry and would neither want nor care about your orange. However, if the prospect hadn't eaten in two days, then she would have an interest in your orange – not necessarily because it's an *orange*, but because of the things the orange can do for her in her state of hunger. And the reality of the situation is that if you were selling a *banana* to her she would be equally as interested because she's not looking for an orange *per se*, but is instead looking for something that addresses her problem of *hunger*.

PART TWO: THE MEAT

The fact that your product is an orange is irrelevant to the customer, and that's the point to be made here: THE CUSTOMER IS NOT AS INTERESTED IN YOUR PRODUCT AS YOU THINK THEY ARE. Customers are interested in the value your product can provide (the orange's nutritional value and sustenance) in helping them address their business problems (hunger); they are not interested in the product (an orange) itself. And remember that value is relative. It's in the eye of the beholder. Your customer decides whether something is of value to them — not you or your company. If they perceive something to be valuable, then it is.

So, in this example, is the orange valuable? Yes, only in the sense that it provides the benefit of *satisfying hunger*, not because it is an *orange!* So as they say: "Sell the sizzle not the steak!"

"Painful as it may be, a significant emotional event can be the catalyst for choosing a direction that serves us — and those around us — more effectively. Look for the learning."

LOUISA MAY ALCOTT

CH09.

I'LL TAKE THE RED MEAT, PLEASE!

"COFFEE IS FOR CLOSERS ONLY!"

QUESTION: HOW DO CONSUMERS BUY THEIR MEAT – BASED ON WHAT CRITERIA? Answer: Based on the *color* of the meat. Not the general *quality!*

Research consistently shows that consumers rank the *color* of the meat as the most important factor that influences their choice of which meat to buy. People prefer their meat to be colored bright red. There is a problem with this because as soon as meat is cut and packaged for sale, there are natural changes that occur and, as a result, the color of meat changes to brown. This color-change limits the shelf life of fresh meat products (people don't like the brown color, so retailers have to reduce the price), even though it does not affect the eating quality of the meat. Scientists are working on ways to overcome this problem, including the addition of antioxidants to inhibit or slow down the color change.

The same applies to other foods, such as salmon. Did you know that they dye salmon to make it more appealing in color (read the fine-print on the label sometime)? Why? Because people believe that the brighter-colored salmon is more fresh and tasty than the naturally-colored salmon product. So, salmon farmers and others dye the fish to make it more sellable to consumers.

If you were a meat or salmon salesman and you didn't know this, you would be at a disadvantage to the competitor that understood these criteria and sold to these reasons why and how people buy meat and salmon. The same concept holds true for other products and services. If you know how and why your customer makes his or her purchase decisions, you would be better positioned to win the business than if you continued to product-pitch and get bogged down in spec wars.

PART TWO: THE MEAT

I'll be the first to admit that finding out why customers make their purchase decisions can be a challenge, and the less comfortable a customer is with the sales rep the less likely the customer will be to share the real reason(s) why. Some customers see the sales rep as someone they have to begrudgingly deal with and, therefore, will never disclose their true buying motivations. It should be obvious to salespeople that most purchase decisions are based on more than one reason, and the more of these so-called reasons you can uncover and sell to, the greater your odds of winning business.

HOW CUSTOMERS MAKE BUYING DECISIONS

Before getting into "why" customers buy stuff, it's important to consider "how" customers make purchase decisions. Psychologists and sales gurus alike agree that customers make purchase decisions on two levels: *logical* and *emotional*.

Logical decisions are made on such things as product specifications (specs), speeds & feeds, price and other tangible criteria of the sort.

Emotional motivations include things that give us a sense of comfort, security, achievement, etc. For example, many years ago I bought a fancy sports car. My motivation was *emotional* (it looked cool, and maybe some of that *cool* would rub off on me), and not *logical* (I have no idea what the horsepower is in the car). If you were trying to sell me a car and all you talked about was the torque, and the horsepower, and the drive train, and the fuel injection, I would tune-you-out because those were not the criteria on which I was making this purchase.

"COFFEE IS FOR CLOSERS ONLY!"

Lots of studies have been done over the years in an attempt to better understand how customers make purchase decisions. The results of these studies are similar and generally suggest that customers primarily make purchase decisions based on *emotion* not *logic*. The *emotional* reasons often include:

1. JOB SECURITY: The decision will help them keep their job and progress in their company, including financially

2. CONVENIENCE: The decision is the comfortable, easy decision to make

3. PEACE OF MIND: Confidence in the decision that it is a safe choice

4. RECOGNITION: The decision will earn the customer props

These decision processes are all based on emotion—how the purchase decision will affect the customer personally. Remember the old saying that "No one has ever gotten fired for buying IBM?" One reason is because many years ago it was hard to argue with the choice of buying an IBM mainframe computer, for instance. Customers knew that they would even be supported tremendously by IBM if a problem occurred – it provided convenience and peace of mind.

WHY CUSTOMERS MAKE BUYING DECISIONS

The question is: why does *your* customer buy products, services and solutions? As I stated previously, it can be difficult to find this out depending on the level of your relationship with the customer.

Several years ago a consulting firm conducted a poll of IT managers to understand why these decision-makers typically made purchase decisions. The general feedback showed that

PART TWO: THE MEAT

product specs were not even in the top-10 reasons:

1. GOOD RELATIONSHIP WITH THEIR SALES REP – they like him/her

2. COMPANY REPUTATION

3. TRUST IN THE SALES REP

4. COMFORT DEALING WITH THE SALES REP and the company

5. THE PRODUCT OR SERVICE will provide some unique value

6. THE PRICE IS FAIR (but not necessarily the lowest)

7. COMFORT WITH THE SOLUTION (knowledge)

8. VALUE IN DOING BUSINESS WITH THE COMPANY and the person they are buying from

This list supports my earlier contention that fewer sales are being made based on product spec wars. And if you think about the reasons why customers buy near-commodity devices like personal computers or paper products or even cell phones, I would argue that it's because of the reputation of the manufacturer's products and comfort knowing that the products will work as desired – convenience and peace of mind.

Whether or not you agree with these findings or any other reports that reveal a customer's reason for making purchase decisions, one thing you will find to be consistent is that for certain products – especially those in the technology sector like PCs and printers and portable music players and cell phones where hardly anything is truly unique — customers rarely make purchase decisions based on product specs (think: why did you buy that iPod?). And if that's true – which I believe it is – then why do sales reps spend so much time presenting this to customers? Insecurity? Lack of skills? Who knows? That's another topic of discussion.

WHY CUSTOMERS *DON'T* BUY FROM YOU

I think it's just as important to understand why your customer is *not* buying from you as it is to understand why they make their purchase decisions. I saw a research report recently that explained why customers typically don't buy from their sales reps. The two reasons that stood out were: (a) The customer doesn't understand the value of what the rep is selling, meaning — how it applies to their business-related issues; and (b) The customer doesn't trust the sales rep.

Putting all of this into context, you will begin to see why I believe sales reps are not being productive by spending their customer sales meetings presenting product features and spec comparisons to any customer who cares that much about them.

More and more, companies are beginning to focus sales training on understanding *how* and *why* customers make purchase decisions, and spend less training time on detailed product knowledge and *"how-to-sell"* sales training.

"Credibility is like virginity. Once you lose it,
you can never get it back."
UNKNOWN

CH10.

CREDIBILITY

PART TWO: THE MEAT

YOU'RE SHOPPING FOR A RACING BICYCLE BECAUSE YOU WANT TO TRY YOUR HAND AT CYCLING. You go to Bobby's Bike Barn where you are greeted by a young 19 year-old salesman who's fresh out of high-school. "May I help you?" the salesman politely asks. "Yes," you answer, "I'm just getting into cycling and I want to buy a good racing bike." The young salesman says, "Umm ... ok, I think we've got some of those over here." He then goes on to try to describe one of the bikes: "This one looks pretty rad, dude! It's a ... umm ... (he reads the tag) ... Trek Livestrong Madone SL." You walk away from the store thinking that the young punk kid doesn't know a THING about racing bikes, and you grow cautious about buying it from him thinking that he'll sell you a bike that's not right for you.

Before making your purchase decision you go next door to Ken's Kool Bike Shop. When you enter the store you're greeted by none other than Tour de France Champion, Lance Armstrong! You describe to Lance what you want to do and he nods and says, "Say no more. I know what you need." He points you to a racing bike and says, "This is your bike! It's a Trek Livestrong Madone SL."

Given the two scenarios, from whom would you feel more comfortable buying the bike? Why? The obvious answer is Lance Armstrong because when it comes to cycling and bikes he is very credible, and a buyer would consider it a safe decision to buy the bike that was recommended by someone who you believe and trust when it comes to cycling.

"Credibility" is the quality of being believable or trustworthy. It is the believability of a statement, action or source, and the ability of the observer to believe that statement. A "credible"

person is considered expert (experienced, qualified, intelligent and skilled) and trustworthy (honest, fair and caring). And a credible source of information can facilitate a quicker more comfortable decision by the buyer. Knowing this, it's easy to understand why having credibility with customers is so important to sales representatives.

There are generally considered to be four types of credibility: *presumed*; *reputed*; *surface;* and *experienced*.

PRESUMED CREDIBILITY. "Presumed Credibility" describes how we ascribe credibility to someone based on assumptions we make about that person. For example, most people assume their church pastor or priest tells the truth, so they view them as credible sources of information. On the contrary, people assume car salespeople are not always truthful and, therefore, lack credibility. The negative view of car salespeople is a stereotype, but that's the essence of presumed credibility; assumptions and stereotypes contribute to credibility perceptions.

REPUTED CREDIBILITY. "Reputed Credibility" describes how we ascribe credibility to a person based on that person's reputation and what other people say about that person.

SURFACE CREDIBILITY. "Surface Credibility" describes how we ascribe credibility to a person based on what we initially observe about that person. The way people dress or the language they use influences our perception of their credibility. That's why I believe a sales rep's degree of neatness and articulation are important.

PART TWO: THE MEAT

EXPERIENCED CREDIBILITY. "Experienced Credibility" describes how we ascribe credibility to someone based on first-hand experience. When we can witness – first hand – the job a person does for us, we are able to form our own opinions of how competent and trustworthy a person is.

Because of history and the legacy of snake-oil salesmen and "quick-buck artists," sales reps inherently have a general and often-undeserving reputation as being something less than trustworthy. It is, therefore, so important to win the confidence and trust of your customers if you hope to build a successful business relationship with them. In other words, it is vital to be seen as a trustworthy resource to your customer, and therefore, it is vital to establish credibility early. But that can be the tricky part.

Credibility can be hard to establish but easy to lose. In some cases, sales reps take months and even years to establish a level of trustworthiness, respect and credibility in the eyes of their customers. But just as it can take years to establish credibility with a customer, it can take only minutes to lose it, and once lost it can be difficult to recover. The easiest and quickest way to damage your credibility? Don't deliver what you promise.

THE CREDIBILITY GAP

The term *"Credibility gap"* was originally a political slogan used in the 1960's to describe then-president Lyndon Johnson's statements about the Vietnam War — there was a "gap" between his administration's statements about the status of the war and what the reality of the war showed. Eventually the term came to represent the difference between what someone states as "fact" and the reality of a given situation — or common sense.

That "gap" between what you promise and what you deliver is also commonly referred to as a *"credibility gap"* (see Table B below). If you have a credibility gap in your customer's opinion, then closing deals with that customer can be quite difficult. Failing to deliver on your promises can also take the form of exaggerating the benefits of a product or service and having that product or service fail to live up to the exaggerated claims.

Imagine you walk into a car dealership looking to buy a fuel-efficient 2006 Honda Civic SI. The car salesman walks up to you and begins to tell you all of the wonderful things about the car: it gets 32 miles-per-gallon highway, it's reliable and it's safe. But then the salesman tries to go for the close and says that because the car is so small and light, that it can be faster than a Porsche 911 GT2 from zero-to-60!

Even if you are not a car buff you should greet that statement with skepticism based on common sense. The Honda's zero-to-60 speed is 7.2 seconds, while the Porsche's zero-to-60 speed is 3.2 seconds. At the moment the car salesman makes that outrageous claim he has lost credibility with you, the potential car buyer, and at that point anything he says to you related to your purchase of that — or any other — car will be disregarded and he will be considered untrustworthy. The result: you'll probably buy from someone else.

PART TWO: THE MEAT

ESTABLISHING CREDIBILITY

So how do you establish credibility with customers? What do you get when you cross an elephant with a rhino? The answer to both: *eliphino!* (I know it's corny, but I love that joke!). But there are some general tips that I and other consultants believe can enhance one's credibility.

- **BE RESPONSIBLE.** Deliver what you promise and take responsibility for your actions.
- **EXPLAIN YOUR COMPETENCE.** Highlight your qualifications. Make the customer aware of your relevant experience and credentials to give them the comfort that you can get the job done — just make sure to do so in a manner that's not braggadocios.
- **BE HONEST WITH YOUR CUSTOMERS** — even when it's painful to do so. Trust me – customers know when you're being deceitful. And don't exaggerate excessively – they can sense that, too.
- **DEMONSTRATE THAT YOU HAVE THE CUSTOMER'S BEST INTEREST AT HEART** and that you are both interested in the success of your customer's endeavor – even though you work for different companies.
- **BE CONFIDENT AND ASSERTIVE.** Nothing spells in-credible like a subordinate, uncertain, timid sales person.
- **LEVERAGE THE CREDIBILITY OF OTHER PEOPLE.** Highlight the credibility of your sources of information. Get introduced by someone who has established credibility with your customer.

And if none of that works, become a *meat inspector!*

"COFFEE IS FOR CLOSERS ONLY!"

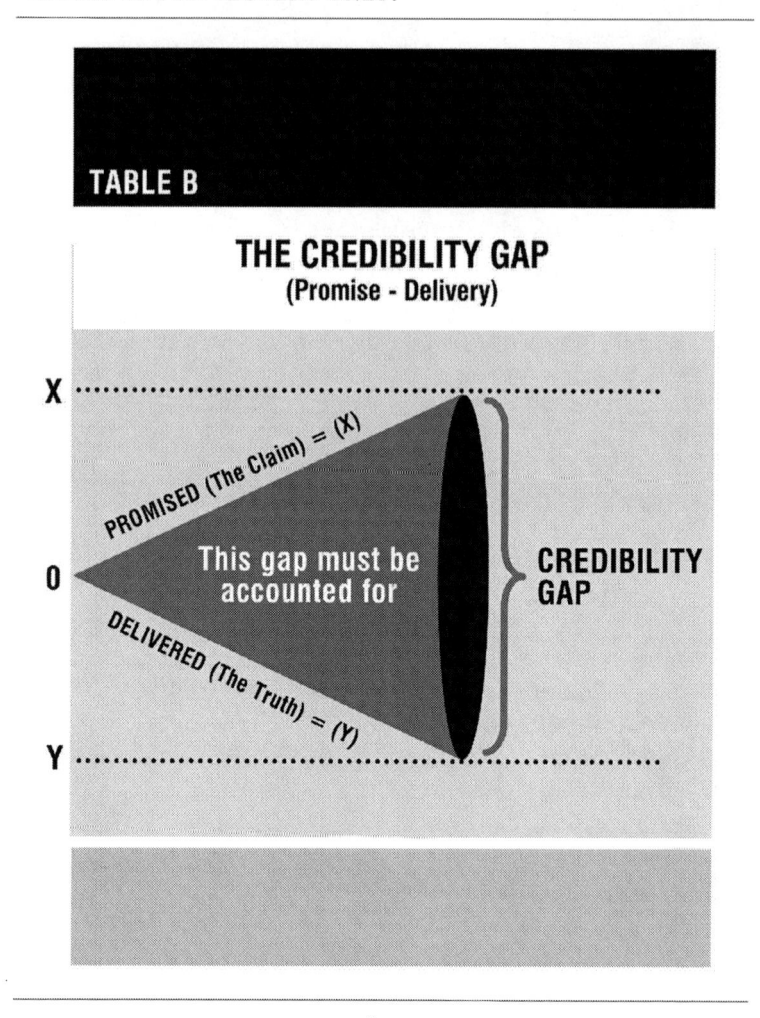

TABLE B

THE CREDIBILITY GAP
(Promise - Delivery)

X ....

PROMISED (The Claim) = (X)

0   This gap must be accounted for   **CREDIBILITY GAP**

DELIVERED (The Truth) = (Y)

Y ....

"First impressions are often the truest, as we find (not infrequently) to our cost, when we have been wheedled out of them by plausible professions or studied actions. A man's look is the work of years; it is stamped on his countenance by the events of his whole life, nay, more, by the hand of nature, and it is not to be got rid of easily."

WILLIAM HAZLITT, British Writer, (1778-1830)

CH11.

HAIR, HANDS & FEET

PART TWO: THE MEAT

THERE'S AN OLD SAYING AMONG SINGLE MEN that you can instantly tell a lot about the quality of a woman by looking at three things: Her hair, her hands, and her feet. And if these three things are not "in order," then, theoretically, a guy should remove this woman from consideration as a potential girlfriend or a future wife. Sounds ridiculous, doesn't it? But believe it or not, a high percentage of single men swear by this rule-of-thumb.

Why, you ask, do men follow such a bizarre rule-of-thumb? After all, a woman is more precious and complex than just the sum of her hair, hands and feet, right? I agree. And I imagine that most men do, too — even those that subscribe to this rule-of-thumb. The theory goes that if a woman spends the time necessary to style her hair or to at least make sure that it is *presentable*, then that is a sign that the woman has self-respect, cares about her appearance, and that she values her partner and her relationships; these are all things that men look or in a potential mate. Oh wait ... it gets better!

If a woman has clean, nicely-cared-for or manicured hands — with clean finger nails — and clean feet & toes (especially the toes), then that is a sign that the woman cares about hygiene. The rationale is that if a woman doesn't take the time to wash her hands — the very things that she eats with, greets with, and are visible all throughout the day, then she's not going to take the time to wash *anything!* (I told you it gets better). Also, if a woman cares enough to make sure her feet are well-cared-for or pedicured — even in the Winter season when her feet are hidden from the general public — then that is a sign of a real "lady."

"COFFEE IS FOR CLOSERS ONLY!"

Hey ... Don't get mad at me! I'm just the messenger; I didn't make this stuff up. But as hard as it may be to believe, most guys that I know use this cave-man screening process when they first meet a woman; that's right, some guys believe that within the first 2-minutes of meeting a woman, they can determine whether or not the woman is a good long-term partner prospect.

And such first-impression-screening techniques are not exclusive to men; women do it, too. I've heard lots of women say that when they first meet a guy they look for telltale signs of a man's "worthiness." For example, some women say that they can tell a lot about a man by looking at his *shoes*. Others say that they can determine if a man is worthy of their phone number by looking at his *smile*, or his *watch*! Whatever the method, the reality is that people form long-lasting impressions of others — within seconds or minutes of meeting a person — based on some set of criteria that they believe are valid indicators of person's *quality*. This is also true in the business world.

In *Chapter 16: "Fishing,"* I offer the suggestion that a sales rep should always be "presentable" when meeting with customers, because — rightly or wrongly — customers are human, and they, too, form initial impressions of the sales reps calling on them based on the sales rep's appearance. In fact, I know some customers who say that when a sales rep walks into their office for the first time, they instantly form an opinion of how "good" that sales rep is based on the sales rep's appearance: Is his or her shirt clean? Do their hands look like they've been working on a car? You get the idea ...

PART TWO: THE MEAT

And whether you buy into this line of thinking or not, there is evidence that suggests people *can* form relatively useful conclusions of a person's work-desirability within the first couple of minutes of meeting that person.

A couple of Harvard psychologists conducted an experiment to try to determine what made teachers effective. Was it body language, appearance, or other non-verbal cues, they wondered. The psychologists gathered some videotape footage of several Harvard graduate student teaching fellows in action. They planned to show the silent video clips to a group of people and have the people rate the teachers based on how effective they believed the teachers to be.

The problem was that the video footage showed the teachers interacting with the students, and the researchers believe that if the reviewers saw this interaction, it would influence their rating of the teachers. However, the researchers found that they could get ten-second clips of each teacher's footage which showed no student interaction. So, the researchers asked the reviewers to rate the teachers along a list of fifteen qualities, based solely on the silent ten-second video clips.

The researchers repeated the experiment using five-second video clips of the same teachers, but asked another group of people to rate them. What they found was the ratings from the group that watched the five-second video clips was identical to the ratings from the group that watched the ten-second video clips! Then, the researchers asked yet another group to rate the same teachers based on a two-second video clip. The result? The ratings were basically the same.

But the most interesting finding resulted when the researchers compared the 10-, 5-, and 2-second video clip ratings to the ratings of the actual students that participated in the teachers' classes for an entire semester. In the latter case, these students knew a lot more about the effectiveness of the teachers since they were taught by them for months. And, surely, these students knew more about the teachers than anyone who simply watched a short video clip. But guess what? It didn't really matter; the ratings by the strangers who rated the teachers based solely on the video clips were almost the same as the ratings of the students that attended the teacher's classes! In other words, people in this experiment formed opinions of the teachers after watching 1 2-second video clip. Or, put another way, people can form relatively accurate judgments of others based simply on a 2-second interaction. Scary!

Since then, another experiment was conducted which applied this concept to the job interview and hiring process. A team of graduate students trained two interviewers on how to apply traditional interviewing techniques and conduct job interviews. When the interviewers were fully-trained, they proceeded to interview ninety-eight prospects. Each interview was about twenty minutes long, and the interviews were video taped. When the interviews were completed, the two interviewers then rated each of the interviewees.

Then, the researchers edited the 20-minute video taped interviews down to fifteen-second clips showing the interviewee entering the room, shaking hands with the interviewer, and taking a seat. That's it! And guess what ... When a group of strangers rated the interviewees based solely on the handshake, their opinions were quite similar to the two trained interviewers who had spent 20-minutes with each candidate! In other words, by the time the interviewee said "hello," an opinion had already been formed by the interviewer about that candidate.

Just like the "hair, hands and feet" rule of thumb described earlier, and the two aforementioned video tape experiments, I believe that customers use their own set of biases and form initial opinions of sales reps when they first walk in the door. We all do it. Everyone has an initial set of prejudices that we ascribe to people at first sight, and customers are no different.

Knowing this, doesn't it make sense to always be "presentable" when meeting with your customers — especially for the first time? After all, you are a *representative* of your company, and oftentimes, the impression you make on your customer is the impression the customer makes of your company. And if you're a single man looking for a wife, buy some good shoes. And if you're a single woman hoping to land Mr.. Right, then remember: Hair, Hands & Feet!

"You never open your mouth until you know what the shot is."
RICKY ROMA, *Glengarry Glen Ross*

CH12.

SHUT THE F@#K UP!!

a.k.a.
THE PANIC OF
THE INTERROGATED

"COFFEE IS FOR CLOSERS ONLY!"

I DON'T MEAN TO BE CRUDE WITH MY CHOICE OF LANGUAGE USED HERE, but let's be honest – anyone who has ever been on a sales call with a prattling sales rep has, at one time or another, wanted desperately to say to the sales rep: *"Just shut the f@#k up!"*

Think about it: how many times have you been on a sales call, presentation or customer meeting with a sales rep that just talked, and talked, and talked without giving the customer an opportunity to get a word in edge-wise? Or how many times have you been in a customer meeting with a customer who is ready to buy, and the sales rep continues to unnecessarily jabber trying to "sell" a deal that's already sold, as opposed to just getting the order and going home? If you're like most professionals, then the answer is probably "too often."

Poor and inexperienced sales reps talk too much. Period. They just don't know when to shut up. Experience shows that when a sales rep talks incessantly, it's a sign that he or she is uncertain about the customer's position, panics, and believes that he/she must continue to try to "tell" the customer even more "good things" about the product being pitched in hopes of convincing the customer to buy it. This is a sign of inexperience. I refer to this phenomenon as "The Panic of the Interrogated." It goes something like this ...

IMAGINE THE SCENARIO: a guy gets busted by the police for some petty crime — say, possession of marijuana with the intent to distribute. And let's assume it is the first time this person has been arrested.

The police officer takes him down to the precinct, throws him into an un-air-conditioned room, beams a hot light down on

PART TWO: THE MEAT

him and begins his interrogation. The officer say to the man, "Ok, perp, what were you doing with the drugs?" That's all he says. Then he sits back silently, arms crossed, and awaits an explanation. Immediately, the guy goes into overdrive trying to explain why he had the drugs on him and how he's not a criminal: "Ya see, officer, I had no idea the drugs were in my pocket! These are my friend's pants ... I was in a fight with some dude, and while we were wrestling around on the ground he slipped the drugs into my pocket ... my girlfriend was mad at me for dating her girlfriend and she put them in my pocket to set me up ... I just bought these pants from a thrift store and the drugs were in the pocket when I bought them ..." [That's another problem when you talk too much — you forget what you said earlier and may start contradicting yourself].

But for all of the guy's explaining, the police offer is unmoved as he sits silently in his chair, arms still folded, and a smirk on his face that says "I'm not buying it." So, what does this inexperienced criminal do? Because he is not sure if the officer is buying his explanation, he panics and talks some more, and more, and more ... Needless to say, all of this talking is not going to change the police officer's opinion of why the guy had the drugs in his pocket. The officer's decision was made way back at the beginning when the criminal first started talking; anything the criminal said after the first couple of sentences was simply a waste of breath and would in no way change the officer's mind.

Now compare that *inexperienced* criminal's approach with that of the *experienced* crook that has a long rap sheet. Same scenario: the police arrest a man for possession of marijuana

"COFFEE IS FOR CLOSERS ONLY!"

with the intent to distribute. They take him down to the station, throw him into that same hot room and begin their interrogation. The officer asks, "Ok, perp, what were you doing with the drugs?" The experienced criminal replies: *"Kiss my ass! I want to talk to a lawyer."* And that's the end of the conversation. You see, the criminal with the experience *knows* when to talk and when to shut up. He knows that the police officer has already made his decision about the drug possession and that nothing the criminal says will change his mind or do any good; all that's left is to get down to business and move this process to closure – get me a lawyer and let's start the negotiations!

That's a difference between an inexperienced sales rep and an experienced rep. The experienced rep has been there before and he or she knows that at a certain point, the customer is going to form an opinion and make a decision — verbally or not. And at that point, no more selling (additional talking) is going to help. All that's left is to ask for the business, close the deal and - *get me a lawyer and let's start the negotiations!*

For most salespeople, shutting-up and listening is difficult. And shutting-up when the customer is non-responsive can be even more so; silence in a conversation makes folks uncomfortable. Consider:

The Japanese style of negotiation incorporates silence as part of the strategy. Japanese negotiators learned long ago that Americans get uncomfortable when their Japanese counterparts sit in silence after the American negotiators have offered a proposal. So what happens? After a few minutes of utter silence, the American negotiators start to get nervous

74

PART TWO: THE MEAT

(besides, it's almost time for their flight back to America) and feel that the Japanese negotiators aren't buying their proposition. So they *start talking* and offering up even *more* perks. Eventually, the Americans will have talked themselves outa everything just because they didn't know when to just *shut the f@#k up!*

It's an ancient rule of selling but it's fundamentally valid - *let the customer talk!* The more the customer talks, the more the customer is likely to provide you with insight that can help you win the business (or help you make the decision that there is no deal there). The more the customer talks the greater the odds of you uncovering the *true* requirements to which you should be selling. And believe me – the more a customer talks, the more the customer will *talk!*

And when a customer starts to open up to you it can be a measure of how comfortable the customer is with you. And the more comfortable they become talking with you the more comfortable they become with *working* with you — it helps build trust! And if the customer *trusts* you then you have achieved a major milestone in the salesperson-customer relationship. So do your self a favor and just remember when to *shut the f@#k up!*

PART THREE

INTERMISSION

"Make your life a mission, not an *intermission*."
ARNOLD H. GLASGOW

CH13.

INTERMISSION

PART THREE: INTERMISSION

A MAN RACES HOME AND BURSTS INTO THE HOUSE, SHOUTING OUT TO HIS WIFE "Sweetheart, I've just won the lottery! All six numbers, $10,000,000! So pack your bags!"

"Wonderful!" says his wife "Shall I pack for the beach or for the mountains?" "I don't care!" The man says, "Just *get the hell out!*"

PART FOUR

THE LOGIC

"Attraction is not a choice."
DAVID DeANGELO, *Author*

CH14.

HOW'D HE GET *HER!?*

PART FOUR: THE LOGIC

BE HONEST. WE'VE ALL SAID IT OR THOUGHT IT. Whenever we see a 5'2" decidedly "ugly" guy walking hand-in-hand with a 6-feet tall super-model, we scratch our heads and wonder: How'd he get HER!? And at that point our imagination starts to take over and we begin to rationalize how such a troll could possibly land a beautiful woman like that. I say we "rationalize" because — let's face it — the thoughts that we come up with as to how the troll possibly got the super-model (he's rich, she's desperate ...) are designed to make us feel better about ourselves in light of the fact that WE can't even get a super-model!

But in the end, I think it boils down to the likelihood that the troll just has *"It."* What is *"It"*? "It" is whatever the super-model was looking for at the time she met the troll, and the troll gave her the assurance that he could deliver *"It."*

Although I've seen this situation play out numerous times, there is one guy who I consider the poster-child for "How'd he get HER!? His name is "Tim" – "Ugly Tim," as we — his friends — call him. [Of course, I've changed his name here to protect the innocent]. Tim is UGLY! There's no two ways about it. He's so ugly that when hen he was born his mother took one look at him and said, "I'll love him anyway." But some things about Tim are attractive: he has the "gift of gab," he's well-read, he dresses nicely, he listens, and he understands the human psyche.

For instance, Tim was once on a local TV dating show competing with two other men for the affections of one woman — kinda like *The Dating Game*. Well, when the three men came out onto the stage, the crowd began snickering when Tim walked out. And when he introduced himself the crowd began

"COFFEE IS FOR CLOSERS ONLY!"

to boo! He was not the crowd favorite. He was short and ugly, but I must admit — he was wearing the absolute most dapper Ozwald Boateng suit I had seen!

So the show begins and the bachelorette starts asking the three men various questions. It became obvious after the 3rd question or so that Tim was a man of substance and somehow knew all the right things to say in response to the bachelorette's questions; the audience loved his answers! So much so, that by the end of the show, Tim was the crowd favorite and was ultimately selected by the bachelorette. And when he waked out from behind the curtain to meet her she took to him like he was *Brad Pitt* and not Ugly Tim!

The old adage was that whenever a Tim-Ugly guy was seen walking with a super-model, everyone thought "he has to either be well-endowed or rich." And even if he was well-endowed, he STILL had to, at some point, approach the super-model, gain her acceptance to talk, and hold her interest. And I sincerely doubt that he just walked up to her and said, "Hi, I'm Tim," and then just whipped-it-out! And if he had money, same thing – I doubt if he just walked up to her and said, "Hi, I'm Tim. Want some money?" No, the truth is that whatever his circumstance, Ugly Tim had to approach a stranger and sell himself as someone she "wanted to do business with." And that always begins with the conversation.

Sure, I acknowledge that there are times when an Ugly Tim may be famous and/or has a reputation that precedes him, thus facilitating his introduction to beautiful women. This would make his connection with the super-model much

PART FOUR: THE LOGIC

easier. But famous people only account for about 2% of the population, which means that 98% of the time, Tim is starting from scratch. And I've seen him in action many times; it's something to behold!

For instance. One evening Tim, some friends and I were in a nightclub. As guys often do, we scouted the joint for the most attractive women. Although there were many in attendance that night, none caught our attention more than this ravishing woman with movie-star good looks (I acknowledge it: we were shallow back then). There we were, four quasi-successful well-educated bachelors and we were ALL reluctant to approach this woman — all, that is, except Ugly Tim.

Tim was *fearless*, and the fear of rejection was not in his DNA. He approached the woman, tapped her on her shoulder, and when she turned around to see who it was, we all saw a look of fright come over her face as though she was thinking "Eew! I KNOW your ugly ass is not trying to talk to *ME!*" Butt then something unexplainable happened. Tim politely apologized for disturbing her, whispered something in her ear, and — like magic — the woman started blushing and laughing! They talked for a few more minutes and then Tim grabbed her by the hand and escorted her over to our table! Huh!? He asked her to join us, and we all just sat in amazement as Tim went to work. It was *masterful!*

It was revealed that this woman was Scandinavian, and Tim would ask her meaningful questions such as: "Are you in support of all of the press that Lene Gammelgaard has been receiving for being the first Scandinavian woman to reach the peak of Mount Everest, or are you saddened that such exposure

"COFFEE IS FOR CLOSERS ONLY!"

is commercializing Everest and tempting other women with a potential danger?" Huh!? We all had absolutely no clue what Tim was talking about, but the woman responded with awe. "Oh my gosh! *Lene Gammelgaard is my HERO!* ..." It was amazing. And as the woman spoke, Tim just listened intently and appeared to genuinely absorb every word the woman was saying. It was an interesting pattern: Tim would ask a question, the woman would talk for several minutes answering the question, and Tim would listen only to respond with another, equally relevant question.

Periodically, Tim would make sure the woman was comfortable and would buy her drinks or snacks if she wanted. Then the conversation would continue. After about 45-minutes of listening to Tim and the woman chat like school-mates, I noticed that the woman was beginning to take-in other aspects of Tim. She would comment on how great his suit was, how sweet he was and how much fun she was having with him. By this point we had had enough and decided to leave Tim and the woman at the night club.

The next day I bumped into Tim and the woman at a shopping mall — they were holding hands like a couple of lovebirds! And almost every guy they passed would have an expression on his face which suggested he wondered: How'd he get *HER!?*

Salespeople can learn a lot from guys like Tim because Tim possesses qualities that make for effective sellers — in fact, what Tim does is sell *himself* (definitely not his looks). A good salesman exudes charisma — people want to be associated

PART FOUR: THE LOGIC

with him or her. The likeability-quotient (or "Q-rating" as it's known in the entertainment world) is always high with the sales reps that form strong relationships with their customers. Customers just like these people. In addition to a high Q-rating, Tim does a lot of things when selling himself that sales professionals should do, and he has many of the same characteristics in his selling motion. Consider:

- Cold calling skills (he approached an apprehensive stranger and engaged her in discussion)
- Communication skills (he's a smooth talker and very eloquent)
- Knowledgeable on many topics (he's very well-read on many topics)
- Not being afraid of rejection (he approached an intimidating, apprehensive stranger)
- Asks for the order (he and the woman were holding hands in a mall the next day)
- Listening skills (he genuinely cares about what people have to say, and it's obvious)
- Probative questioning skills (he asks the questions that get people to open up)
- Uncovers what's truly important (he's a great probative questioner and intense listener)
- Compassion and empathy (he feels your pain)
- Neat appearance (he's ugly but well-groomed and wears

Ozwald Boateng suits)
- He's smart (he has a MBA degree and is a voracious reader)
- High Q-rating (people just like him)
- Credibility (according to the ladies, he delivers what he says he will!)

Knowing this about Tim, it becomes less of a reach to understand how he meets so many beautiful women. Tim is not afraid to ask for the "business." And you'd be amazed at how many "customers" are just waiting for ANYONE to bring forth a compelling "solution" to their true immediate "needs."

"A little nonsense, now and then,
is relished by the wisest men"
WILLY WONKA

CH15.

A SERIOUS VEXATION

.PERSONALITY·TYPES ANALYSES &
SELF·PROFILE·ASSESSMENTS

PART FOUR: THE LOGIC

SORRY, BUT I'VE JUST GOTTA GET THIS OFF MY CHEST. Some psychiatrist or psychologist or grade-school teacher or consultant looking to cash-in on the naievete of unsuspecting sales managers or ... whatever ... woke up one day and apparently decided there was some value in irrationally identifying the "type" of person someone is — based on a questionnaire — and incorporating that "profile" into one's sales efforts. In other words, they are trying to teach sales reps how to categorize people and form oversimplified conceptions and unsubstantiated opinions of someone without knowing that person — isn't that the definition of *"stereotyping"*?

Can you believe this! Some training consultants are actually propagting the use of profiling and stereotyping! What's worse is they expect salespeople to use this meaningless information in selling situations. The whole notion just seems wrong to me. This is the kind of nonsense that results when you try to psychoanalyze the art of selling. Now ... before I continue, I KNOW that I'm gonna get a lot of hate-mail from sales trainers and consultants who disagree with my opinions in this chapter. I'm sure they'll claim that: "You just don't understand." Maybe not, but since this is *MY* book, I can write whatever I want.

IT GOES SOMETHING LIKE THIS: Psychologists have developed different tests that are supposed to place people into groups based on their response to the questions contained in the tests. The questionnaires used are typically either the kind you used in high school (where you darkened the oval with a #2 pencil) or multiple-choice questions containing a list of items to select from. These assessment questionnaires ask you a series of

"COFFEE IS FOR CLOSERS ONLY!"

questions about how you do things, such as: "When making spaetzle do you use salted water?" or "When you use the bathroom, do you look before you flush?" Based your answers to these questions, you are placed into a group. Usually these groupings are few, and each group has characteristics associated with them. So, depending upon which group you fall into, you are supposed to have the characteristics of that group — *profiling* and *stereotyping*.

For instance, one of the personality-type tests that everyone uses identifies people as "Type A" personalities or "Type B" personalities. A person that is characterized as *Type A* is supposed to be high-strung, animated, aggressive, outgoing, etc. A *Type B* person is said to have the opposite characteristics: laid-back, easy going, etc. According to the logic of people who develop these tests, *everyone* will fall into one of these two categories. Preposterous, ain't it? People are more complex and have more dimensions than that.

I once went on a job interview for a software company and they made me fill out one of these assessments. After completing it, the sales manager began to tell me about myself based on my answers to the questions on the questionnaire. He even began to make judgments about my potential for success based on the questionnaire. The manager then said: "So ... I see here that you are an introvert and prefer to work in groups ..." At that point I thought of how ridiculous the whole thing was and walked out on the interview, leaving the sales manager puzzled. My thinking was: why would I want to work for a company and a manager that places stock in that nonsense?

PART FOUR: THE LOGIC

Another popular personality-type indicator tool is the Myers-Briggs tool. This test goes a little further and places people into one of several categories, including: Extroverts (E), Introverts (I), Sensors (S), Intuitives (I), Thinkers (T), Feelers (F), Judgers (J), and Perceivers (S). What facilitators of the Myers-Briggs course say is that the tool develops a representation of a person's preferences and salespeople can use these personality types (which dictate preference) to know what each "type" likes and dislikes, how they should be dealt with, and to make judgments about people based on the group they fall into. They even go so far as to encourage salespeople to fill out a questionnaire choosing the answers they believe *their customers* would choose, and decide which group their customers would fall into. Then, they say, you will be more effective in your sales efforts with these customers because you will know their personality-type and how to deal with them. *i'm not kidding!*

This is like asking an Asian salesperson who has never interfaced with African-Americans to do an assessment of his African-American customer using whatever information he has heard about African-Americans as a guide for completing the questionnaire. If this Asian salesperson grew up in Montgomery, Alabama during the '60s and has a negative perception of African-Americans, will his assessment of his customer have any value? NO!

I know this is an extreme example, but I use it to make the point that regardless of what you think a person is like based on some unnatural group they are "placed into," you can't use such information to help you interact with that person. This is

"COFFEE IS FOR CLOSERS ONLY!"

especially true in the sales environment.

When I completed the Myers-Briggs type indicator questionnaire (for the fifth time! Some companies go overboard with this) my latest typing was "ISTP." Keep in mind that I came out with a different typing each time I completed one of these questionnaires (Hmmm, does that mean I have multiple personalities?). Anyway, after everyone was categorized, the instructor went around the room and told each person what he/she was like, based on their type.

When she got to me, she said, "You're an 'ISTP' and that means you pay no attention to deadlines, you focus on the present, objectify time and you play and work together." HUH! What does that mean!? At that point, I couldn't pass up the opportunity to ask the million-dollar question. I asked the instructor: "Excuse me, but even if that was correct, SO WHAT?!?"

After getting over the shock that someone would actually question the usefulness of Myers-Briggs, the instructor mumbled, "It's just something to keep in your back pocket." In other words, she was saying, "You suckers spent a whole day going through a useless exercise!"

I also found it entertaining that my personality-type chart stated that I *analyze facts impersonally* and that *I analyze facts personally*. Go figure.

I don't know of any one who has ever used these types of assessments for anything except entertainment value – or an easy way to get out of the office for a day. It's one of those things that you sit through and, when you're done, you throw

PART FOUR: THE LOGIC

all of the materials from that class into a drawer only to re-discover it years later when you're cleaning out your desk — and then you throw it in the trash! Is that what companies intend for salespeople when they hold these sessions? I think not.

Here's a simple test you can perform to determine whether or not you really buy-in to the usefullness of these types of tools:

SCENARIO 1: You go to a job interview and the interviewer doesn't ask you any questions, but instead, asks you to complete a profiling questionnaire. You complete it, hand it in, and the interviewer says "Thank you for coming. I'll take a look at your profile and let you know whether or not I want to hire someone like you. Bye!" Would you be comfortable with that? If "no," then *why not?*

SCENARIO 2: You finally get that big meeting with the Vice President of your big account. You walk into her office and she asks you to fill out a profiling questionnaire. You complete it, hand it back to her, and she says, "Well it was nice to finally meet you! I'll take a look at your profile and then I'll decide if you're the kind of person I want to do business with." Would you be comfortable with that? *Why not?*

I try not to be a person that wantonly offers criticism without explaining the basis for my criticism or the rationale behind my position. So, you ask, why do I have such a negative opinion of these courses? Because, in my opinion, the whole concept falls down when held to a higher level of scruiting. Here are some of the challenges:

SELECTIVE PERCEPTION AND WEAK HYPOTHESES

In science the process goes something like this: (a) In an attempt to understand, we develop a hypothesis (or multiple hypotheses) or a theory about why something is the way it is or how something works. (b) We then gather information, data and/or evidence that either supports or refutes our initial hypothesis. (c) We confirm, modify or reject our hypothesis based on the new information.

Most consultants and other lay-folks who create these profiling courses would make bad scientists becayse they — like people in general, fall prey to "selective perception" and tend to only see what they are looking for and to overlook data which is not specifically included in their search plan. They tend to limit the information that is compiled to that which is relevant to their current hypothesis.

So, if the consultants form a hypothesis that says: *By asking 20-questions to sales professionals we can understand their selling characteristics. Then, we can use that information to make recommendations on how they can improve sales* — then any research that comes back which doesn't support their hypothesis will be rejected, as opposed to forcing them to develop alternative hypotheses. When information is processed in this manner, it is easy to "confirm" almost any hypothesis that one already believes to be true. Believe it or not, this happens all the time — even among real scientists.

In the absence of a complete set of alternative hypotheses, it is not possible to evaluate the "diagnosticity" of evidence that supports their hypothesis. Unfortunately, consultants

PART FOUR: THE LOGIC

(and many analysts) are unfamiliar with the concept of *diagnosticity of evidence*. It refers to the extent to which any item of evidence helps the analyst determine the relative likelihood of alternative hypotheses. If it were measured in the case of profiling assessments, the diagnosticity would be weak and the hypothesis would have to be rejected. Or to put it in layman's terms — the whole idea would be considered *bulls@#t!*

INSUFFICIENT INFORMATION

All of these profiling assessments are designed to yield information about a person that can be used to form opinions of someone and even to base decisions on. The profiling questionnaires contain questions that are limited and generic, which means that any information derived from these questionnaires would be insufficient in truly understanding a person. Insufficient information increases uncertainty and hampers the decision-making process.

Like I said earlier, people are complex and multi-dimensional. As such, it would be very difficult to capture the essence of a person from a questionnaire — especially from a *short* questionnaire. There's a type of behavioral assessment called the DISC Profile that asks about 28-questions — yes, very short. They ask you to select from a list of questions those things that *most* represent you and *least* represent you. Here's an example:

From the list of items beow select the ONE item that most represents you. (By the way, you MUST select one of the choices provided below!):

"COFFEE IS FOR CLOSERS ONLY!"

- [ ] If I don't get my way, I'll cry and throw a temper-tantrum
- [ ] If I don't get my way, I'll beat my cat
- [ ] If I don't get my way, I'll hold my breath until I pass out
- [ ] I always get my way, whether I'm right or wrong!

From the list of items beow select the ONE item that least represents you. Remember, you MUST select one of the choices provided below!

- [ ] I have respect for others
- [ ] I wish for world peace and the end of poverty
- [ ] I am fairly intelligent
- [ ] I enjoy eating food when I'm hungry

It's easy to see the problems with this type of assessment. Most obvious is the fact that the limited choices offered might not represent the respondent if he or she is forced to choose one of the supplied answers. But even after you go through this entire process and determine your and your customer's type, *so what!?* Do they really expect anyone to use such foolishness on a sales call? I can see it now: "Hmm. Based on my D-I-S-C assessment of this customer, he is a high "D" and a low "I" so I'd better deal with him in this manner and ask these types of questions." You've gotta be kiddin' me, *right?*

I don't believe that any worthy sales rep would even think about applying that technique on an actual sales call. When sales reps are in the middle of a sales call, they will inevitably interact with that customer based on instinct and the natural flow of the discussion.

Retired Stanford University professor and author, Alexander George, has done seminal works on topics of policy and decision-making. He has identified a number of less-than-optimal strategies for making decisions in the face of incomplete information (yep, that's profiling assessments) and multiple, competing values (yep, that's profiling assessments, too). While George conceived of these strategies as applicable to how decision-makers choose among alternative policies, I and many others believe that most also apply to how analysts might decide among alternative hypotheses.

The relevant "less-than-optimal" strategies George identified include:

"SATISFICING" — Selecting the first identified alternative that appears "good enough" rather than examining all alternatives to determine which is "best." In our DISC (or other) profiling questionnaires, this is what respondents are being asked to do. But most importantly, these questionnaires cannot offer enough choices of answers in a questionnaire that would provide enough profile alternatives to formulate the truly "best" profile of a person. If so, the questionnaire would contain 1,000 questions. And did I mention *selective perception?*

"INCREMENTALISM" — focusing on a narrow range of alternatives representing marginal change, without considering the need for dramatic change from an existing position. In this case, the profilers focus on a narrow range of alternatives representing very marginal characteristics of a person. And did I mention *selective perception?*

CONSENSUS — opting for the alternative that will elicit the greatest agreement and support. Simply telling the boss what he or she wants to hear is one version of this. Another is responding to a survey in a manner that we believe people want to see. Yet another is creating a profiling assessment that forces people into neat little compartments by offering a limited set of choices; this makes it easier to explain to customers and offers cute little buzzwords to throw around. And did I mention *selective perception?*

REASONING BY ANALOGY — choosing the alternative that appears most likely to avoid some previous error or to duplicate a previous success. Sounds familiar, doesn't it?

THE USE OF QUESTIONNAIRES

There's so much heavy competition in the training and consulting fields today, that you see many examples of questionnaires (developed for specific engagements) with little research and no statistical analysis of their reliability or validity. In these cases, they are more marketing tools than anything else, and the results they yield are often useless because the claims made of these questionnaires often exceed the limits of their development.

Because questionnaires create data which represent models of reality, they must be seen for what they are: a simplification and reduction of reality (the operative words here are *simplification* and *reduction* of reality — how do you reduce

PART FOUR: THE LOGIC

reality, anyway?). And that's how they gain their popularity, by claiming to boil life down into a few compartments with catchy buzzword labels.

Because they are boiling down an infinite amount of information into bite-sized chunks, they must at some point force-fit data into the compartments where it wouldn't otherwise fit. It is therefore incumbent on consultants and trainers to clearly and honestly explain to their participants the limitation of the models they are using. And if this was ever done honestly, then no company would waste their money doing it!

One big problem with using questionnaires of any type — especially profiling assessments — is *"response error."* Response error is the difference between the true answer to a question and the respondent's answer. Think about it: how many times have you completed questionnaires where you were not totally honest with your responses or where, because of confusion, you selected an answer that was misrepresentative? We all have.

Another of my concerns is with the *relevance* of the data that the design of the questions yields. The *relevance of data* is a quantitative assessment of the value contributed by the data. *Value* is characterized by the degree to which the data serves the purposes for which it was produced and requested by participants. Participants take these profiling courses to help them sell more stuff, and for all of the reasons I describe in this chapter, profiling assessments and their associated questionnaires don't help you sell more stuff. My conclusion: there is little-to-no *value* in the data so it's not *relevant*.

MEASUREMENT

Simply put, *measurement* is a logical rule for assigning numbers to observations to represent the quantity of a trait or characteristic possessed. Or, in the case of profiling assessments, it assigns values to questionnaire responses in order to represent a trait or characteristic of a person or people.

So, if the measurement is wrong or poor, then it stands to reason that the resulting representations are wrong or poor. I'm sure the profilers would argue that what they have developed are *qualitative* models and not *quantitative* measures — to which I say: same concept.

There are many ways a measure can be wrong. Let's see how many of these items apply to profiling assessments.

- Poor construct validity (yep, especially with regard to hypothesis testing and questionnaire development)
- Low reliability (yep, for all the reasons I describe above)
- Lack of precision (yep, this is pretty obvious)
- Data is too expensive or impossible to collect (too expensive — no. Impossible to collect — maybe. I contend that people are so complex and multi-dimensional that in order to develop an assessment methodology and the associated questionnaire that would accurately capture the essence of a person, it would require thousands of questions which no one would complete. Hence, no sale!)
- Difficult to use (No. Hey ... whaddaya know?!)
- Not a good predictor (Yep, and that's my whole point!)

PART FOUR: THE LOGIC

I'm sorry to hit you with so much heaviosity in this otherwise light-hearted book, but this is a pet-peeve of mine that I just had to get off my chest. [Inhaling ...] *Ahhh!* Now I feel much better! And I just saved myself thousand of dollars on therapy!

"Advice is what we ask for when we already know the answer but wish we didn't."

ERICA JONG, American writer and feminist

CH16.

FISHING!

"COFFEE IS FOR CLOSERS ONLY!"

AS HARD AS I TRIED TO DELIVER THIS BOOK WITHOUT INCLUDING ANY OF THOSE "HERE IS WHAT YOU SHOULD DO TO BE A GOOD SALESPERSON AND INCREASE YOUR SALES" TYPES OF RECOMMENDATIONS, the publisher insisted that I do just that. So ... under durress, I caved.

One reason why I am usulply reluctant to tell sales reps that they should follow a rote set of selling steps like — *do A-then-B-then-C in order to improve your sales performance* — is because, to me, that stuff is for entry-level sellers trying to learn the fundamentals of selling, and not for experienced sales reps. Not only that, but most of those recommendations are a waste of time. In my opinion, making sales is a lot like *fishing*: it ain't all skill, technique and process.

Catching a fish and closing a sale are both a result of several conditions that must be present in order to be successful. It involves a combination of skill, available prospects, opportunity, territory conditions, your supporting cast (depending on the size of the fish) and the tools available to you. Consider the parallels: (See *Table C* below)

To test my belief that making a sale typically requires multiple conditions to be present and favorable, do the following: remove each condition listed in the table below except *skill*, and then determine whether the odds of your selling success will go up, stay the same or decrease. I contend they will decrease *dramatically*.

Now, start adding each condition back into the equation one-by-one, and notice how incrementally better your odds appear the more you add those conditions back in. As I said earlier, making sales is about more than just following some process or employing some methodology that's "guaranteed to increase your sales." And that is why I don't like to give salespeope the impression that their sales will increase by simply following some step-by-step approach, because I believe it's about more than that.

However, the publisher holds the purse-strings and, as a result, I am a hired hand. So — begrudgingly — I'm gonna offer my thoughts on a few things that I think can help you in selling situations. But before I get to that, I want to review a few market shifts that are making it more challenging for today's sales professionals to close deals than at any time in history.

SALES ARE BECOMING MORE COMPLEX

In the go-go 1990s when the economy was strong, many companies' idea of a strategy was to buy as much *stuff* as they could afford, whether it was technology hardware or tallow. And then the roof caved in and companies were stuck with excess expensive inventory and, in many cases, excess capacity.

To avoid a recurrence of this sort of binge-spending and its damaging aftermath, companies are now requiring more diligence in the buying process, including in-depth analyses and detailed business cases that include convincing ROI. Business case development requirements have increased the complexity of the buying process by, for instance, requiring that more people become involved in the process.

In addition, there are more complex product offerings and more competitors competing for the same conservative purchasing budgets. All of this has resulted in more complex deals, longer sales cycles and a requirement of more consultative selling skills.

"COFFEE IS FOR CLOSERS ONLY!"

TABLE C: Fishing vs. Selling

CONDITION	FISHING	SELLING
1 SKILL	If you are skilled and knowledgeable enough to know that floating fly line with a mayfly dun tied to the end of a long and fine leader is not the best way to catch big fish, then – all things being equal – you will be more successful then the fisherman who doesn't.	If you're a seasoned salesperson that has had years of varied selling experiences, has credibility, and knows how to sell and move the sales process forward, then – all things being equal – you will be more successful that the sales rep that is an inexperienced order-taker.
2 AVAILABLE PROSPECTS	If you want to catch big fish you have to go to where the big fish are. I don't care how skilled a fisherman you are – if you're fishing in a lake hoping to catch a shark, it ain't happenin'.	If you want to sell a Rolls Royce you have to have an available market of wealthy prospects. If you set up shop in Beverly Hills you will have more success than if you located in Cleveland.
3 MARKET CONDITIONS	The time of day, time of year and weather conditions can have an effect on the degree of success you achieve when fishing.	A company's financial performance and the conditions of the market they are in can determine their degree of spending and affect your success.
4 OPPORTUNITY	When fish (typically in the salmon family) leave lakes or the salt water to spawn, their movements can be predictable, and the more concentrated they become, thus increasing your odds of a bountiful take.	If you sell security services and all of your prospects have just entered into 2-year agreements for Security Officer on-Site services from your competitor, then you're not going to be very successful selling yours.

PART FOUR: THE LOGIC

TABLE C: Fishing vs. Selling (continued)

CONDITION	FISHING	SELLING
5 SUPPORTING CAST	Ever tried to catch a 12-foot Great White shark by yourself?	Depending on the product or service being sold, sales professionals often require the support of subject-matter experts, legal representatives, administrators, product experts and others to successfully close a deal.
6 TOOLS	Depending on what you are fishing for, your odds of success can be increased by matching our equipment to your targeted prey, and by using the latest technologies.	Imagine you are going head-to-head for a deal against your most formidable competitor. Now imagine that the only tools and technologies you have at your disposal are a pencil and an abacus. No PC, no cell phone, no software tools, nothing. Tough, ain't it?

109

"COFFEE IS FOR CLOSERS ONLY!"

In the past, a high percentage of sales transactions were completed in a *transactional* manner because the products were simpler, there were fewer decision-makers involved in a deal, fewer sales calls were necessary to close a deal, relationships were less important, and sales reps could actually get away with using some of those *"do-A-then-B-then-C"* sales techniques to move a deal forward.

Today, buyers are tighter with the purse-strings and are making purchase decisions more cautiously. The selling terrain is highly-competitive and much more complex to navigate. Products and services are more complex, more people are involved in the buying/decision-making process, risks for the customer are higher, and there has been a shift from *price-based* decisions to *value-based* decisions. And in order to successfully navigate this terrain, sellers are required to adjust their paradigm and to be more consultative in their approach, and relationships are more important now than ever.

This is why companies want their sales reps to become more strategic, consultative sellers and less tactical product-peddlers. *Consultative Selling* is a whole separate book topic in and of itself, so I won't really get into that here. However, the following tips should help sellers interact with customers more effectively in this brave new world of complex selling:

TIPS

1. **BE OPEN AND HONEST WITH YOUR CUSTOMERS**, no matter how painful. You have to forge a respectful, professional relationship with your customers so that you can discuss difficult topics and ask the hard questions without fear of

110

chastisement. And don't be afraid to deliver bad news in a timely manner; this is more appreciated by customers than not doing so.

2. **IN INITIAL CUSTOMER CALLS AND MEETINGS, TRY TO APPROACH THE CALL AS IF YOU HAVE NO PRODUCTS, GOODS OR SERVICES TO SELL.** In other words, if you couldn't talk about the stuff you had for sale, then how would you approach the meeting? It forces the discipline to really spend the time listening to the customer.

3. **BE PRESENTABLE.** Rightly or wrongly, some customers make credibility judgments about you based on how you present yourself when they first meet you. This isn't to say that you have to show up at your customer's office wearing Dolce & Gabbana, but just keep in mind that you are a representative of your company, and the impression you make on your customer is often the impression they will form of your company. Or, think of it this way: if you were going to a customer meeting along with the President of your company, how would you present yourself?

4. **KNOW OF WHAT YOU SPEAK, OR DON'T!** Few things can hurt one's credibility more than speaking on subjects about which you have no knowledge. Far too often sales reps try to tap-dance their way through questions raised by customers, when both the sales rep and the customer know that the sales rep doesn't know the answer. No one knows everything, so there's no shame in not knowing everything that a customer will ask of you. Besides, customers know when you're bulls@#tting them, and it's not a good look.

5. **ASK FOR THE BUSINESS!** More than ever it appears that sales reps are, for some reason, reluctant to ask customers for the business. Can you stand it!? Apparently, *closing* has become a lost art. Although it is so fundamental a sales activity, many sales reps neglect to perform this most important of activities. Failure to ask for the customer's business is one of the reasons sales reps don't get their business. It can also contribute to a longer sales cycle which can, in turn, lead to a lost deal for many reasons.

6. **DON'T GIVE AWAY ANYTHING FOR FREE WITHOUT GETTING SOMETHING BACK IN RETURN.** It's simple negotiation. It helps put you on even footing with the customer, and it lets the customer know that what they are asking for has value. In addition to being a good business practice, it can also serve as a qualification point; if a customer is serious about doing business with you, they should be willing to comply.

7. **DON'T DISPARAGE THE COMPETITION TO YOUR CUSTOMER.** There is no good that can come out of it. For one thing, the customer won't believe you anyway because you're a competitor of the company you're disparaging. In addition — and even more damaging — the statements you make about your competitor are probably incorrect! This can make you appear untrustworthy to the customer and you run the risk of alienating that customer from doing future business with you. And besides ... it's *bush league*.

8. **CONDUCT RIGOROUS DEAL-LOSS REVIEWS.** The way some companies react when their sales reps lose a deal would give you the impression that, "It's okay that you lost that deal.

We'll get the next one." It shouldn't be "ok" to lose a deal, and when a deal is lost, companies should work diligently to understand what went wrong, why, specifically, the deal was lost, and to put plans in place and make adjustments to ensure that no other deals are lost for that/those reason(s).

Effective deal-loss reviews are frightening inquisitions for the sales rep because, if it is revealed that the loss was due to a mistake by the sales rep, the sales rep would face unpleasant consequences. Or, if the sales rep did everything correctly, then the reason for the loss would be addressed. Effective deal-loss reviews involve input from the customer (such as the real reasons why the deal was lost) and participation by the sales rep's management organization.

9. **CONDUCT ANNUAL FULL-YEAR SALES PLANNING WORKSHOPS.** This cornerstone of account planning forces the sales team to formulate a plan — at the beginning of the year — that shows how they plan to achieve their sales goals for the year. It should involve participation by each member of the extended account team, action items, ownership and due date commitments should be assigned, and the plan should be managed-to and adjusted throughout the year as appropriate.

10. **BE HONEST WITH YOURSELF.** Be honest about everything from the quality of the deals you are pursuing to your ability to get a deal closed without help. If you can't do that, then you can never be honest with your customers and you will

inevitably do your company a disservice.

You will notice that most of the aforementioned Tips have to do with *credibility*, which, in my opinion is one of – if not the most important characteristics of a sales professional. So, in other words, my main suggestion is to work to establish and maintain credibility with your customers.

"This is the very perfection of a man, to find out his own imperfections."

SAINT AUGUSTINE

CH17.

CHARACTERISTICS OF THE PERFECT SALESPERSON

PART FOUR: THE LOGIC

"COFFEE IS FOR CLOSERS ONLY!"

PART FOUR: THE LOGIC

"The greatest friend of truth is time,
her greatest enemy is prejudice, and
her constant companion humility."

CHARLES COLTON

CH18.

TAB'S FIVE UNIVERSAL TRUTHS

"COFFEE IS FOR CLOSERS ONLY!"

THROUGH ALL OF MY YEARS OF INVOLVEMENT IN THE SALES ARENA, there are certain things that have proven to be universally true:

1. You're not as good as you think you are
2. Making quota hides a lot of sins
3. The customer is not as interested in your product as you think they are
4. Nobody likes to deal with SALES PEOPLE!
5. Nobody really "loves" to sell, and if they tell you they do, they're lying!

UNIVERSAL TRUTH #1:
YOU'RE NOT AS GOOD AS YOU THINK YOU ARE

Former NFL (National Football League) Head Coach, Mike Ditka, lead the Chicago Bears to a Super Bowl championship victory in 1985. Coach Ditka was considered to be an outstanding coach, and I'm sure that every other non-Super Bowl team in the league would have loved to have him as their head coach.

It stands to reason that when you lead a team to such a dominant championship victory you will inevitably start to believe your own press and — even if subconsciously — begin to think that you were the main reason why the team won the championship.

In 1992, Mike Ditka would eventually leave the Chicago Bears and become the head coach of the woeful New Orleans Saints in 1997. He spent three years coaching the Saints and amassed a record of 15 wins and 33 losses. In the process, he inexplicably traded away several draft picks to acquire former

PART FOUR: THE LOGIC

University of Texas running back, Ricky Williams. When Coach Ditka left the Saints, how many other teams were courting him to be their head coach? Zero!

So, does the fact that Mike Ditka — the former Super Bowl Champion coach — couldn't win in New Orleans mean that he was never a good coach after all? I don't know, but I don't think that's the case. But what I believe it did show Coach Ditka was that he was probably not as good a coach as he thought he was back in 1985.

It's just like selling: you may be a good sales rep, but even the best of sales reps need certain "positive" conditions to be met before they can win big, including a support staff, administrative processes, accounts or a territory where real opportunity exists, viable products or services, properly set sales goals (quotas), etc. If these positive conditions are met, then any good sales representative is going to be successful nearly every time.

However, if some of these conditions are not met, then even the brightest sales reps can fail. The bottom line is that even though you may be considered a "star" sales rep in your company, the reality is that you are only as good as the opportunity with which you are presented and the support system behind you to help you be successful. If the conditions are bad, then you will perform poorly. Does that mean you are a poor sales rep? No. But, remember — in many companies, you're only as good as your last year's performance, and if you have a couple of bad years in a row – even if these bad years are a result of poor conditions in your assignment — your reputation as a star sales rep will become somewhat tarnished.

"COFFEE IS FOR CLOSERS ONLY!"

The big difference between a good sales rep and a poor sales rep, however, is that even when the aforementioned "positive" conditions are present in a poor sales rep's assignment, he or she will oftentimes still be unsuccessful. Or, as an old friend and former sales colleague of mine, "Honest Cheech," would say: "You can take one account from any sales rep and RUIN 'em!" Touche! And if you don't believe it, try it on yourself: think of your most significant account or customer and remove them from your list. Now ask yourself, "Without this account/customer in my patch, will I have a good year?" The answer is usually NO!

And another thing: You're only as good as your last year's Performance.

If ever there was a profession where the question, "What have you done for me lately?" is applicable, it's sales. You're in good shape as long as you are making your annual quota. However, when you miss your quota for a year, people start questioning your ability.

How many times have we as sales managers said: "Yeah, John is awful ... the worst! But I couldn't fire him last year because he made his quota, and I can't fire him now because he's making his quota." And then we begin to track John's performance – waiting for that one quarter when he doesn't hit his numbers so that we can fire him!?

Sales managers have short memories. They can't remember — and frankly don't care — what you did two years ago. They must be kept satisfied year-to-year. So, if someone is not contributing to their satisfaction, the sales manager would

PART FOUR: THE LOGIC

just as soon hire someone else.

Today, most companies don't value the non-financial value a salesperson brings to bear his or her territory; it's mostly about the numbers. You're a star until you miss quota one year, and once you do, your name will most likely end up on the chopping list. Conversely, you can be a loser for your whole career, but if you're hitting your numbers this year, then — short of getting caught stealing your CEO's Mercedes Benz — you will live to see another quota cycle.

UNIVERSAL TRUTH # 2:

MAKING QUOTA HIDES A LOT OF SINS

In this day and age where sales performance is often measured on a quarterly basis, managers are under more pressure to deliver results than at any point in history. In many companies it has reached the point where making the sales quota is all that matters. Oh, you say you wanna be treated as a human being? Like more than just a *revenue-generating conduit?* Then go work for the Peace Corps because, in corporate America, the numbers are what matters most, it seems.

An issue with this *quota-at-all-costs* mentality we are faced with today is that quota-attainment is often the only performance measurement used in employee performance reviews. Of course, no company will admit that, but deep down inside we all know it's mostly true.

I say this is a problem because the quota-attainment measurement has become the de-facto criteria for lazy managers to use in determining who their "star" sales reps are. Far too

"COFFEE IS FOR CLOSERS ONLY!"

many managers today have absolutely no clue about how genuinely good their sales reps are at the art of *selling*. Instead of taking the time to truly understand the degree to which their sales reps understand the process of selling, their mastery of the deal-pursuit process and their foundational knowledge of the fundamentals of how-to-sell, today's managers will simply look at the year-end numbers and say ridiculous things like, "Oh, I see that Joe has sold $2 Million worth or products and has attained 300% of his quota last year; the highest in the company! So he must be the best sales rep in the company— a *star!*"

For example, John Doe is a salesman for ABC Software Company. John has never had any sales training, has never held a sales job before and is a terrible communicator. In short — John has absolutely no clue how to *sell* anything. However, because he has a family relative high-up in the company, he landed a sales rep job managing a global account.

John got his assignment at a great time because his customer would be upgrading their software system over the next 2-years. So, as soon as John took over the account, his customer began ordering millions of dollars worth of software. All John had to do was process the orders when they came in. In his first two years John maxed out at 500% of quota each year and made a ton of money! Because of his outstanding quota performance, he is declared to be the best salesman in the company and is promoted to sales manager. All of a sudden, ABC Software Company finds itself with a sales manager that doesn't know how to sell. And as a result, John hires other salespeople that don't know how to sell because John

PART FOUR: THE LOGIC

doesn't know what to look for in a "good" sales rep. The cycle perpetuates.

The fact that John brought in some big numbers blinded the greedy managers to the fact that he is not a good salesman; in fact, he's the *worst* salesman in the company but is being called the best. Look around you. I'll bet that you see examples of this in your own company.

Many managers today don't seem to care how a sales rep achieved such outstanding numbers as much as they care about how much money that sales rep has made them; and for that, they are ever so grateful. Therein lies the problem: if your company's sales organization is not performing against the industry as effectively as you believe it should be — yet, most of your sales reps are still hitting their quota — then either you have superior sales reps across the board, or sales assignments, metrics, targets or other criteria are not set properly. But since everyone is achieving their quota targets, no one is looking beneath the covers to learn why the sales organization's reps are not more effective account *managers*.

UNIVERSAL TRUTH # 3:

THE CUSTOMER IS NOT AS INTERESTED IN YOUR PRODUCT AS YOU THINK THEY ARE

[Also see Chapter 8: *Selling an Orange*]

If I asked the question: *Why does your customer buy your products?* I would be willing to bet that 90% of sales reps' answers will have something to do with a feature or technological aspect/specification (spec) of the products. This *product mentality* is quite common — especially in technology sales — but it's also antiquated because, truth-be-told, a small percentage of (technology) decisions are based solely on product specs and features. Think about it. If product specs and features are the reasons customers make purchase decisions, then none of us would have VHS format video machines – we'd have BETA machines; no one would be using IBM format personal computers – we'd be using Macs; no one would be using the Internet Explorer web browser — we'd be using Mozilla Firefox. The list goes on.

Have you ever asked yourself, "Why do companies buy *Brand X* products when *Brand Y* products are 'so much better'?" And don't delude yourself by thinking that price is the only reason — it ain't!

Customers buy for reasons that infrequently have to do with product features per-se, especially in a product segment that is becoming commoditized like paper products, PCs and raw materials. And customers don't buy for the reasons that you want them to buy for; they buy for *their* reasons. And the higher up the organization chart you go, the less those executive (read: most important) customers care about specific features of a product. They are more concerned with the value those products can deliver which will help them achieve their business objectives.

I know lots of very good, very successful sales professionals, and – to the one – they will all tell you that when they're talking to executives they hardly ever mention a product feature or spec; they focus on what the executives want to know: conceptually, *how can you help me satisfy this business objective?*

When was the last time you called on a line-of-business executive of a *Fortune 500* Company — say, VP-level and above — and they actually cared about all of the speeds, feeds and spec minutia of your product offering? Remember the old saying (ok, ok ... it's not an *old* saying, but it's one that I have been using for quite a while): If you're an account manager and you're spending all of your time talking to customers who care a great deal about product features and specs and how they compare to your competitors', then you're probably spending far too little time talking to those customers that are making the final decision.

UNIVERSAL TRUTH #4:

NOBODY LIKES TO DEAL WITH SALES PEOPLE!

[See Chapter 3: *Run, Hide!*]

UNIVERSAL TRUTH #5:

NOBODY REALLY "LOVES" TO SELL,
AND IF THEY TELL YOU THEY DO, THEY'RE LYING!

[See Chapter 6: *Liar, Liar, Pants on Fire!*]

"The point is that you can't be too greedy."
DONALD TRUMP

CH19.

YOU SHOULD BE OFFENDED!

"COFFEE IS FOR CLOSERS ONLY!"

ANY GOOD SALESPERSON WHO MANAGES AN ACCOUNT SHOULD BECOME TERRITORIAL when it comes to his/her customer. If you are truly concerned about being the absolute best service provider to your customer, then you should be offended when your customer buys from, or considers using the products or services of your competitor(s), specifically when it is a product or service for which your company has a viable solution alternative.

I say this because I believe if you are the "incumbent" provider in the account, and your customer buys a competitor's product — knowing that your company has an equivalent (or greater) product offering — then that's a sign that your customer doesn't have complete confidence in you as a provider of goods and services. It could also mean that your competitor is outselling you in the account. Either way it's not a good thing, and could very well be an indication that you and/or your company are slipping in your customers' eyes.

CONSIDER THIS: You start an eBay business selling soccer balls. In order to ship the soccer balls to your customers, you stock up on 1' x 1' cardboard boxes that you purchase from Bob the Box Guy — a reliable box seller who has been in the box business for 20-years. As your eBay business grows, you buy more boxes from Bob. After only a year in business, your business is booming and the number of boxes you buy from Bob has increased fifty-fold! Things are going fine: you're selling hundreds of soccer balls every month and your box supplier, Bob the Box Guy, who has been with you from the beginning, has always delivered your boxes on-time and at a fair price.

One day, Bob the Box Guy calls you concerned that the size of your latest box order was for a smaller quantity than is

PART FOUR: THE LOGIC

customary. You assure him that everything is okay, that he'll still be your box supplier, but that you decided to buy just a few of the same boxes from another supplier -- Ken the Crate Caterer.

Ask yourself: *"Why would I start buying from Ken the Crate Caterer when Bob has been doing business with me for years?"* What are some of the reasons you would suddenly decide to buy some of Ken's boxes which are practically the same as Bob's? And if you are Bob the Box Guy, how would you feel about your customer buying a similar product from another supplier? That's right, you should be *offended!* And if you're not offended when your customer buys a competitor's product, then you deserve to lose the business because you are not focused on providing such great service to your customer that the customer would have no reason to buy from anyone else.

I remember working as a salesman for a company that believed it was its birthright to supply every one of its customers with all of the technology products and services the customer needed — period! This sense of account "ownership" permeated the company and every sales person considered it an insult if their customer purchased products and services from a competitor; I felt the same way. Why? Because we believed we had the industry's best products and the infrastructure to ensure that we could always satisfy the customers' requirements.

We also believed that we were the best trained sales force with a focus on servicing the customer to death. To us, we believed there was absolutely no reason for our customers to buy a comparable product from a competitor — unless we as sales

"COFFEE IS FOR CLOSERS ONLY!"

reps were somehow not doing our job.

Sure, there are always customers who want the leverage that comes from having at least a couple of vendors they can buy from, but even in these cases, I believed that they would only consider doing something like that because they didn't have 100% trust in me and the confidence that I would only do right by them. Well, I don't believe it was as much a "belief" on my part as a mindset that I had as a young salesperson. My attitude was that I should *never* lose a deal for which I had a viable solution.

In those days, I remember always looking at the sign-in log book at the security desk of my customer accounts to see which of my competitors had been in there and whom they were visiting. Whenever I did see a competitor signed-in to see an "important" manager, I felt betrayed in a sense, and made it a point to stop by that manager's office to find out what's brewing. Wouldn't you?

For some reason, we concern ourselves in our personal lives when this type of thing occurs, but when it happens in our business life, it's somehow okay.

Think about it. You're a working parent who prepares a lovely chicken dinner for your kids, only to hear your 12-year-old say that he'd rather to go over to his friend Joey's house for dinner because Joey's mom is also cooking chicken dinner. Wouldn't you wonder why your son would rather have chicken dinner at Joey's house instead of eating yours? Wouldn't you be somewhat offended?

Or, for instance, if you ask your longtime girlfriend to go with you to the movies to see the midnight showing of *Gone*

PART FOUR: THE LOGIC

With The Wind, and just then her phone rings ... she answers it ... she hangs up ... and then she tells you that that was a co-worker — *Dr. Francois L'Amour* — and he, too, wants to take her to see the midnight showing of *Gone With The Wind*. And then she tells you that she's decided to let Dr. L'Amour take her instead of going with you. Wouldn't you wonder why? Wouldn't you be offended?

Today, I get the sense that most sales reps don't take it personally when their customers buy from their competitors; they consider it to be just the nature of the business. In fact, they don't even get angry when their customers buy "inferior" products from their competitors! Be *offended*, sales people! It's *Dr. Francois L'amour*! Take it personally! Because when you are offended by such actions by your customers, it's a sign that you taking a vested interest in being such a valued and trusted resource to your customer, that your customer would have no reason to do business with anyone else. And when you approach your account management efforts with that mindset, it can't help but to make you a better representative of your company to your customer.

ANOTHER REASON YOU SHOULD BECOME TERRITORIAL in your major accounts is because your account is ... well ... a "territory," and he who *owns* the account rules the territory.

Imagine your account as a territory comprised of many different Pods of Opportunity (POO) as illustrated in the diagram below. A POO is simply a requirement or a need the customer has that can be satisfied by your company or a company in the same industry as yours (i.e. a competitor).

"COFFEE IS FOR CLOSERS ONLY!"

In this account/territory, there are 25 Pods of Opportunity; the more POOs you can satisfy with the sale of a product, service or solution, the more account ownership and control you have. So, if your company has sold the solutions to satisfy 100% of the POOs, then you have total (100%) account control; this is utopia for *all* sales reps.

If only life were that simple. The reality is that there is a competitive battle to "control" the account (have total mind-share with the executive customers), and seize "ownership" of the *territory* (maximum share of the customer's wallet). The goal of all smart sales professionals should be to gain 100% ownership and control of his/her account(s) — the *territory*.

For example, let's assume that each POO has a certain percentage-of-account-ownership & control associated with it based on the bigness of the dollar value of the solution that will be required to satisfy the POO (see the table above). So, if you and your company provided solutions for every POO in the account/territory, then you would have 100% ownership & control; life is good!

If only life were that simple. The reality is that there is a competitive battle to "control" the account (have total mind-share with the executive customers), and seize "ownership" of the *territory* (maximum share of the customer's wallet). The goal of all smart sales professionals should be to gain 100% ownership and control of his/her account(s) — the *territory*.

PART FOUR: THE LOGIC

COMPANY ABC:
TWENTY-FIVE (25) PODS OF OPPORTUNITY

The Territory: Total Opportunity = 100%
If the smaller deals (those less than 5%: highlighted) are all won by competitors, then your ownership & control become weakened and you run the risk of being displaced

Pod 1 6%	Pod 2 4%	Pod 3 4%	Pod 4 2%	Pod 5 4%
Pod 6 2%	Pod 7 4%	Pod 8 7%	Pod 9 3%	Pod 10 4%
Pod 11 2%	Pod 12 2%	Pod 13 2%	Pod 14 4%	Pod 15 10%
Pod 16 1%	Pod 17 1%	Pod 18 15%	Pod 19 2%	Pod 20 1%
Pod 21 4%	Pod 22 8%	Pod 23 3%	Pod 24 2%	Pod 25 3%

For example, let's assume that each POO has a certain percentage-of-account-ownership & control associated with it based on the bigness of the dollar value of the solution that will be required to satisfy the POO (see the table above). So,

"COFFEE IS FOR CLOSERS ONLY!"

if you and your company provided solutions for every POO in the account/territory, then you would have 100% ownership & control; life is good!

Now imagine that your account started buying products, services and solutions from your competitors. The more stuff they buy from competitors, the less account ownership & control you have, the less money you make, and the more indifferent your customer becomes with your level of support of their company. It's almost like a chess game: You want to control as high a percentage of the board as possible to maximize your ownership & control of the game; the more positions (POOs) your competitor captures (wins) and controls, the weaker your competitive position. And the weaker your competitive position, the greater the threat that you will be displaced in the account — Check Mate!

Hopefully, this example illustrates why you should be concerned when your customer starts buying from your competitors — regardless of the size or the dollar value of the POO. If a competitor starts winning enough of the "small" POO deals, they become a threat to slowly increase customer mind-share. This can eventually lead to the competitor winning bigger and bigger deals until, eventually, you and your company have been displaced in the account. BECOME TERRITORIAL!

The bottom line is the greater percentage ownership & control you have of your account, the more money you will make in the account, and — theoretically — the greater the level (measure) of satisfaction your customer will have with your representation.

PART FIVE

THE CLOSE

"Men of quality are in the wrong to undervalue, as they often do, the practise of a fair and quick hand in writing; for it is no immaterial accomplishment."

MARCUS FABIUS QUINTILIANUS

CH20.

CROSS PENS

"COFFEE IS FOR CLOSERS ONLY!"

IF I RECEIVE ONE MORE CROSS PEN AS A SALES INCENTIVE I AM GOING TO JAB MYSELF WITH IT!

At the time of this writing, I had been selling professionally for a total of about twenty-two years. During that time, I have received no fewer than two Cross pens per-year from different companies. Who was the genius that decided a Cross pen was something salespeople would cherish? I have spent many sleepless nights wondering where it all started. Who was the first person in corporate America that decided to give employees the dreaded Cross pen gift? A recent event forced me to wonder about this more than anyone should ever have to.

I was recently cleaning-out my desk drawer and realized that I have accumulated *more than 52 Cross pens* throughout my career! More than FIFTY-TWO!! I say *more than* fifty-two because the fifty-two Cross pens I found in my drawer don't include the pens I have thrown-away over the years. Why did those companies give me all of those pens? Why? Why is it that companies all across America feel compelled to give salespeople Cross pens for a job well done? Throughout my whole career I have never met a salesperson who has said, "Did you hear!? First prize in the quarterly sales contest is a set of Cross pens!! I sure hope I win!!"

No salespeople want them as premiums; they want *money!* No one really seeks them out to use them. No one values them (the gift models, anyway) all that much, and, more telling, I don't know of anyone who *buys* them! (When was the last time you saw a salesperson purchasing a Cross pen? They don't. Why? *Because they get so many of them as sales prizes!*). So

PART FIVE: THE CLOSE

why do companies continue to give them as prizes?

Some companies started getting wise to the fact that salespeople didn't want these "perks" after finding hundreds of black graphite Cross pens in the trash can. A sane person would see this and say, "Hmmm ... maybe we should think of something different to give salespeople." But, instead, the corporate gift-buying person says, "Hmmm ... maybe we should think of something different to give salespeople. I've got it! Instead of giving them those *black graphite* Cross pens which they throw away, let's give them the *golden tone* Cross pen!"

How did it all start? Who was the first person to give them as perks to salespeople? Which company was the first to encourage the profusion of "the rabbit pen" throughout their sales force? I imagine it must have begun something like this...

The A. T. Cross Company was formed in 1846. The original products were silver and gold pencil casings, and the company's founder held the patent on the forerunner of the ball-point pen. The company refers to the Cross pen as a "writing instrument" (they take this seriously). Apparently, they were known for quality back then and it was a big deal to own a writing instrument — not to mention a Cross pen.

I imagine that in the early days of organized selling circa 1900, most salespeople either used lead (pencils) or fountain pens for writing. Along comes the Cross "stylographic" pen (the forerunner of the ball-point pen) and, suddenly, writing with ink was easier, more convenient and less messy. As a result, it was probably a big deal to own a Cross pen. I guess

"COFFEE IS FOR CLOSERS ONLY!"

it was about this time that companies began to issue Cross pens to their salespeople for the status and convenience the pen offered. Not only that, but in 1900 it was probably a great gift to receive. Somehow this tradition has lasted into the 21st century even though, today, owning a ball-point ink pen is commonplace.

Somewhere down the line came the ball-point pen. Suddenly, ink pens became common and very inexpensive. Households now have hundreds of ink pens, whereas in 1900, it was rare for households to own even one. Today, you can get a pack of ten ink pens for fifty cents, and they write just as effectively as a Cross pen. As a matter of fact, my ink pen of choice is the ten-cent *Bic Banana*; receiving a Cross pen just doesn't get me excited.

The Cross company must have one helluva marketing staff because they have convinced corporate America that, even today, a Cross pen is a great gift, a status symbol and something that salespeople crave. Cross must have also cornered the market on catalogue-order writing instruments because when administrative assistants order inexpensive gifts from the corporate catalogue for the sales force, their automatic choice is that damned Cross pen! Enough already!

The cheap-model Cross pens are not a status symbol for salespeople anymore. When a salesperson whips-out a gift Cross pen in front of today's customer, the customer must think, "Oh, he's using a low-budget 'quality' pen. Maybe when he gets some money he'll buy a *real* pen." (Actually, most customers don't care about that, but I'm trying to make a point).

Listen corporate gift-givers: STOP GIVING SALESPEO-

PART FIVE: THE CLOSE

PLE CROSS PENS! They probably have enough of them drying-up in their desk drawers and they don't value them anymore. There's only one corporate gift that's almost as un-fulfilling to receive as a Cross pen, and that's the *paperweight!*

I don't want to give the impression that I think Cross pens are crap, because I don't. In fact, I think the Cross *Apogee* and the Cross *Current* models are very, very cool pens. However, no one is giving those *desirable* pens away.

Lately, though, some companies are stepping-up and are now offering salespeople Mont Blanc pens and Waterman pens. But as the price of these pens comes down, so does their reputation as a status symbol and, ergo, a valued gift. Besides, if we already have a lifetime supply of Cross pens in our collection, why do we need any more pens at all? So maybe you should stop giving ink pens and paperweights altogether. *Foldin' money* will do just fine!

"Life is really simple, but we insist on making it complicated."
CONFUCIUS

CH21.

CONCLUSION

"COFFEE IS FOR CLOSERS ONLY!"

SELLING IS NOT MAGIC. If you listen to some people, you could get the impression that selling is an art form on par with designing a space ship. It's obviously not. And how hard can it be? When you consider how some people with no formal traditional sales training generate healthy incomes without even being able to speak the proper language, you have to believe that it's more than about just *selling techniques*.

I am a firm believer that sales reps go through what I call a *Sales Experience Cycle* (see the table below), and at each stage of the cycle we exhibit different levels of understanding of the selling process, and we can navigate the Stages to the Sale more comfortably and successfully the farther we move down the Experience Cycle.

In the early stages of the Experience Cycle, sales reps participate in fundamental sales training classes, learn their craft, make mistakes, and question why they ever became a salesperson. As sales reps gain more on-the-job experience, they become more comfortable in their jobs to the point where – after a while – they run on *autopilot*: doing the job becomes second-nature and they have a high deal-closure rate. All of the initial sales training they participated in, the mistakes they made, the experiences they gained, and the the key learnings have become ingrained in the seasoned-seller, to the point where the job *just happens*.

I thought about this concept this morning when I was shaving. When I shave, I use shaving powder that must be mixed with water before it can be applied to my face. When mixed with water, the shaving powder becomes a paste which can be spread on your beard area like shaving cream, and then

PART FIVE: THE CLOSE

shaved-off using a spatula.

The shaving powder I use contains lye, so it must be used carefully. I know ... you're asking WHY I would use something like THAT? Well, I use it because it *works the best* for me.

Back to the story ...

I have been using this shaving powder for many, many years, and when I first started using it, I followed the mixing, measuring and application directions very carefully. But even so, I suffered the rookie consequences: I left it on my face too long and burned my face; I spilled some on my arm and it left a spot.

But over time, I became more comfortable using the shaving powder to the point where I have mastered its use; I don't even think about it when I apply and use it — I'm on *autopilot*.

So, this morning when I pulled out the can of shaving powder, I noticed that they changed the label somewhat and added more specific usage instructions. I started reading the instructions (which I hadn't done in many years), and thought: "Huh!? That's not what *I* do!" So, I read on: *mix 2 tablespoons of shaving powder with equal parts water* – I don't do that. I just mix it until it's at a consistency I prefer. *Leave it on your face for no longer than 5-to-7 minutes* – What? I leave it on *much* longer than *that*. *Do not wash off with soap!* – Oops! I have been washing it off with *soap* for over 20-years!

My experience with using shaving powder reminded me of selling: sure, I used to follow the step-by-step "how-to-shave" process when I was new at it. But over time, I developed my own process that works successfully for me — and I did so with the fundamentals of using shaving powder in my back pocket. But I don't think about the "how-to" process anymore; it's ingrained in me to the point where I *know* what to do to achieve the successful result I want.

And that's what happens as we move along the Sales Experience Cycle. We have been trained so much and we gain so many experiences along the way, that we simply *know* how to do the job at a high level, without having to think about such things as: *okay, I've done A-then-B, now what am I supposed to do next?*

Much of selling has to do with the buyer's *comfort level* with the seller. It has to do with quaified opportunities, it has to do with the environmental conditions surrounding the prospect, it has to do with the support infrastructure availale to the seller, it has to do with more than simply following a step-by-step selling methodology.

But there is something that is fundamental to all meaningful sales engagements between buyer and seller, and that's *credibility*. Credibility has to do with likeability, trustworthiness, confidence in the seller, and other such positive characteristics which customers tell us are the reasons they often choose one sales proposition over another.

Another thing that I believe is important to becoming a better seller is understanding why you win and lose deals, and accurately (and honestly) capturing those reasons. If you know specfically why you *won* a deal, capture those winning actions and build upon them for future engagements.

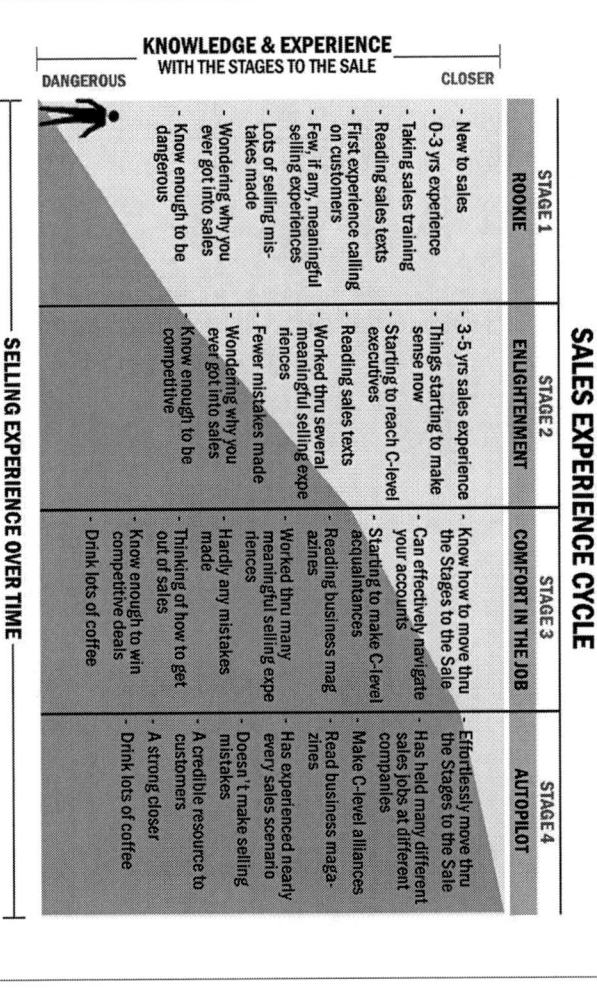

PART FIVE: THE CLOSE

SALES EXPERIENCE CYCLE

KNOWLEDGE & EXPERIENCE WITH THE STAGES TO THE SALE

DANGEROUS — CLOSER

SELLING EXPERIENCE OVER TIME

STAGE 1: ROOKIE
- New to sales
- 0-3 yrs experience
- Taking sales training
- Reading sales texts
- First experience calling on customers
- Few, if any, meaningful selling experiences
- Lots of selling mistakes made
- Wondering why you ever got into sales
- Know enough to be dangerous

STAGE 2: ENLIGHTENMENT
- 3-5 yrs sales experience
- Things starting to make sense now
- Starting to reach C-level executives
- Reading sales texts
- Worked thru several meaningful selling experiences
- Fewer mistakes made
- Wondering why you ever got into sales
- Know enough to be competitive

STAGE 3: COMFORT IN THE JOB
- Know how to move thru the Stages to the Sale
- Can effectively navigate your accounts
- Starting to make C-level acquaintances
- Reading business magazines
- Worked thru many meaningful selling experiences
- Hardly any mistakes made
- Thinking of how to get out of sales
- Know enough to win competitive deals
- Drink lots of coffee

STAGE 4: AUTOPILOT
- Effortlessly move thru the Stages to the Sale
- Has held many different sales jobs at different companies
- Make C-level alliances
- Read business magazines
- Has experienced nearly every sales scenario
- Doesn't make selling mistakes
- A credible resource to customers
- A strong closer
- Drink lots of coffee

"COFFEE IS FOR CLOSERS ONLY!"

If you specifically know why you *lost* a deal, identify those reasons — through a rigorous deal-loss review — put plans in place to ensure that you never lose business for those reasons again, and build on that for future engagements.

Yes, folks, selling is a competitive profession that hardly anyone really enjoys doing. It is fraught with high-turnover, high stress, a "what have you done for me lately?" attitude, and lots of coffee drinking. So, if you have to do it, then I suggest you focus on the common-sense fundamentals and learn from each engagement so that you can move down the Sales Experience Cycle to the point of becoming a seller that's running on *autopilot!*

CH22.

CURTAIN CALL

"COFFEE IS FOR CLOSERS ONLY!"

WHEN THE MILKMAN FOUND A NOTE ON ONE OF HIS CUSTOMER'S DOORS asking for 16 gallons instead of the usual quart, he rang the bell. "Sorry to bother you, ma'am," he said, "but are you sure you want sixteen gallons of milk today?" "Oh, yes," said the lady of the house. "I'm going to take a milk bath." "Do you want it pasteurized?" "No, just up to my chest would be fine."

ABOUT THE AUTHOR

TAB EDWARDS is a consultant and author with over 24-years of experience in sales & marketing, consulting, entrepreneurship and business management. Mr. Edwards earned his undergraduate degree from the University of Pittsburgh, and his MBA degree from the Pennsylvania State University.

He began his business journey at the tender age of 13, selling inexpensive household items door-to-door. Although he has held award-winning sales, consulting and management positions at some of the words most admired companies, including IBM Corporation, General Electric, the Sales & Marketing Consulting Company (SMCC), Gimbel Brothers, and Hewlett-Packard Company, he cites his door-to-door encyclopedia salesman job at Collier's Encyclopedia as the job that taught him the most valuable lessons about selling.

Mr. Edwards shares his breadth of knowledge and experience by working with a broad range of companies including non-profit agencies, small & medium businesses, and *Fortune 500* Corporations.

"COFFEE IS FOR CLOSERS ONLY!"

An Arab sheikh tells his two sons to race their camels to a distant city to see who will inherit his fortune. The one whose camel is *slower* to reach the destination will win. The brothers, after wandering aimlessly for days, ask a wise man for advice. After hearing the advice they jump on the camels and race as fast as they can to the city. What does the wise man say? (Answer below)

HE TOLD THEM TO SWITCH CAMELS

PART FIVE: THE CLOSE

STAGES TO THE SALE

▶ **IDENTIFY A PROSPECT**

▶ **GAIN ACCESS TO THE PROSPECT**

▶ **DETERMINE OR CONFIRM THE EXISTENCE OF AN OPPORTUNITY**

▶ **QUALIFY THE OPPORTUNITY**
- Do I THINK there's an opportunity?
- Do I KNOW there's an opportunity?
- Can I PROVE there's a real opportunity

▶ **UNDERSTAND THE TRUE REQUIREMENTS**
- Do I THINK I understand the true requirements?
- Do I KNOW what the true requirements are?
- Can I PROVE that I know the true requirements?

▶ **DEVELOP POTENTIAL SOLUTION AND JUSTIFICATION**

▶ **QUALIFY THE SOLUTION**
- Do I THINK the sol'n will deliver expected benefits?
- Do I KNOW it? Can I PROVE it?
- DO I THINK the customer will buy the value of the solution? Do I KNOW it? Can I PROVE it?
- Does the customer have funds allocated?
- Have I sold the solution to the signatory?

▶ **PRESENT THE SOLUTION PROPOSAL**

▶ **CLOSE THE DEAL AND GET THE SIGNED ORDER**

OXFORD HILL PRESS

ALSO AVAILABLE FROM AUTHOR

TAB EDWARDS

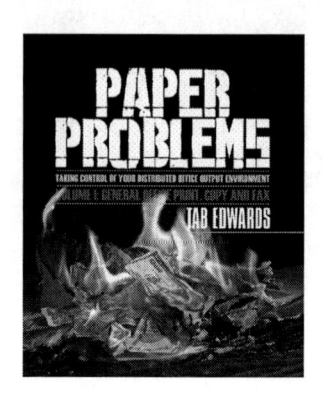

"PAPER PROBLEMS"

THE GUIDE TO UNDERSTANDING AND FIXING YOUR
DISTRIBUTED OFICE PRINT, COPY, FAX AND SCAN
ENVIRONMENT

WWW.OXFORDHILL.COM